William Weeks Morrill

Of the Law and Practice in Actions Against Municipal Corporations

For Negligence in the Care of Highways

William Weeks Morrill

Of the Law and Practice in Actions Against Municipal Corporations
For Negligence in the Care of Highways

ISBN/EAN: 9783337158941

Printed in Europe, USA, Canada, Australia, Japan

Cover: Foto ©Suzi / pixelio.de

More available books at **www.hansebooks.com**

OF THE

LAW AND PRACTICE

IN ACTIONS AGAINST

MUNICIPAL CORPORATIONS

FOR

NEGLIGENCE

IN THE CARE OF HIGHWAYS.

BY

WILLIAM W. MORRILL,

AUTHOR OF "COMPETENCY AND PRIVILEGE OF WITNESSES."

NEW YORK:

S. S. PELOUBET,

LAW PUBLISHER AND BOOKSELLER,

80 NASSAU STREET.

1887.

BY W. W. MORRILL,

1887.

PREFACE.

Actions against municipal corporations for injuries arising upon highways are, it is generally admitted, unduly numerous. To account therefor, some persons argue an unseemly readiness to make cities and villages suffer for the misfortunes of travellers ; others insist that the corporations are quite too forgetful of their duty toward those who use their streets. Probably both opinions are correct.

Irrespective of merit, such actions abound and are to be prosecuted and defended. If they do not constitute a separate title in the law, or deserve consideration in a separate treatise, there still may be room for a hand-book of ready reference to matters likely to arise during their preparation and trial. A desire to provide something of that sort is the motive of this book.

The plan of treatment contemplated at the outset is rather rashly made public in the introduction ; it may promise somewhat too much or too little ; still it is not believed that any striking departure has

[iii.]

been made from the scheme there outlined. To what is there stated may be added, that since the subject under consideration is only a branch of the general subject of negligence, it has been found necessary to consider many topics common to that whole subject, and useful to draw illustrations from the whole field of negligence cases.

Finally, it may be stated, that while the book is primarily, to use the language of the almanac-makers, "calculated for the longitude of" New York, yet the statutes and decisions of other States are constantly cited and considered; and the intention has been to make its application general, so far as may be, without going into all the technical details peculiar to each jurisdiction.

W. W. M.

TROY, N. Y.,
August 15, 1887.

TABLE OF CONTENTS.

PART I.

LAW.

CHAPTER III.

CHAPTER XIII.

CHAPTER XIV.

CHAPTER XV.

PART II.

PRACTICE.

CHAPTER I.

CHAPTER II.

CHAPTER III.

CHAPTER IV.

CHAPTER V.

CHAPTER IX.

TABLE OF CASES.

NEW YORK.

        B.   [xvii]

Page

OUTSIDE NEW YORK.

D

CITY-NEGLIGENCE BRIEF.

PART I.
LAW.

CHAPTER I.

INTRODUCTORY.

1. Scope and limitations.
2. Sources of danger to travelers.
3. Injuries without remedy.

1. Scope and limitations of proposed subject. One who is injured in person or property on the public highway naturally has his attention turned to these three questions:

> Have I a remedy?
> Against whom may I enforce it?
> How shall I proceed?

Some examination of these questions is here proposed; not, however, in detail as to every class of offenders or every locality or jurisdiction.

1

The primary subject of investigation will be the rights and remedies:

> of persons sustaining loss or injury,
> by reason of wrongful or negligent mismanagement of highways,
> by municipal corporations,
> in the State of New York.

To that extent only will any pretense of exhaustive treatment be made.

Incidentally, however, there will also be considered to some extent:

(a) The liability of persons or corporations, other than the municipalities themselves, by whose fault streets are rendered unsafe.

(b) The liability of *quasi* corporations, as counties and towns, or officers thereof, on whom rest a statutory obligation to keep highways safe for travel, and a statutory liability to persons injured.

(c) The rights and remedies of travellers on highways outside the State of New York.

2. Sources of danger to travellers. It is quite unnecessary to dwell on the variety of objects and occurrences which may become sources of mishap upon highways, and may be included within the generic terms " obstruction" and "defect."

Judging from reported cases, the trenches which are so frequently and necessarily opened in the streets of cities, for the purpose of laying water, gas, sewer and other pipes, and the aggregation of ice and snow which accompanies the northern climate, are responsible for a large share of the injuries sustained by those who use the streets of cities and villages.

In addition to these, may be merely mentioned at this point various others, taken at random from the reports.

(a)   Actual obstructions, as

Heaps of ashes,

Ring r. Cohoes, 77 N. Y. 83.

Counter on sidewalk,

Kunz v. Troy, (N.Y. Ct. App.) 35 Alb. L. J. 232.

(b)   Actual defects, as

Broken, misplaced, or uneven curb or flag-stones, or pavements, holes in streets, &c.

Healy v. New York, 3 Hun, 708.
Saulsbury v. Ithaca, 94 N. Y 27.
Goodfellow v. New York, 100 N. Y. 15.
O'Neill v. New Orleans, 30 La. An. part 1, 202.
Hildreth r. Troy, 101 N.Y. 234.
Bullock v. New York, 99 N.Y. 654.
Hines r. Lockport, 50 N.Y. 236.
Russell r. Canastota, 98 N.Y. 496.
Minick v. Troy, 83 N.Y. 514.

Decayed platform over well,,(¹) or displaced(¹) or slippery(³) vault cover.

(¹) Sherwood r. District of Columbia, 3 Mackey, 276.
(²) Smith r. New York, 15 W. Dig. 103.
(³) Stillwell r. New York, 49 Super. 360.
    Cromarty v. Boston, 127 Mass. 329.

(c) Unguarded embankments,

> Flagg *v.* Hudson, (Mass.) 34 Alb. L. J. 279.
> Wyandotte *v.* Gibson, 25 Kan. 236.
> Atlanta *v.* Wilson, 59 Ga. 544.
> Nowell *v.* New York, 52 Super. 382.
> Cummins *v.* Syracuse, 100 N.Y. 637
> Veeder *v.* Little Falls, Id. 343.

(d) Abrupt change of grade of side-walk,

> Koch *v.* Edgewater, 14 Hun, 544.
> Urquhart *v.* Ogdensburg, 97 N. Y. 238.
> Higert *v.* Greencastle, 43 Ind. 574.
> Clemence *v.* Auburn, 4 Hun, 386 ; 66 N. Y. 334.

(e) Objects thrown or falling from above, as

Ice and snow thrown from roof,

> Atholf *v.* Wolf, 22 N. Y. 355.

Or falling from slide leading to ice-house,

> Fleming *v.* Lockhaven, (Pa.) 31 Alb. L. J. 178.

Falling trees,

> Vosper *v.* New York, 49 Super. 296.
> Gubasco *v.* New York, 12 Daly, 192.

Falling brick,

> Rehberg *v.* New York, 91 N. Y. 137.

Falling awnings,

> Hume *v.* New York, 74 N. Y. 264.
> Bolien *v.* Waseca, 32 Minn. 176.

Or bill-boards,

Langan r. Atchison, 35 Kansas, 318.

.

(h)   Causes of fright to horses, as

Heaps of stone

Eggleston r. Columbia T. Co., 82 N. Y. 278.

Banners,

Champlin r. Penn Yan, 34 Hun, 33.

Hole in bridge,

Smith r. Sherwood, (Mich.) 34 Alb. L. J. 119.

Steam motors,

Stanley r. Davenport, 54 Iowa, 463.

Fire-works,

Conklin r. Thompson, 29 Barb. 218.

Carcass of horse,

Fritsch v. Allegheny, 91 Pa. St. 226.

For injuries arising from all these, and numberless other sources of danger, municipal corporations, as well as others, may, under proper circumstances, be liable to those damaged thereby.

The very large class of "running-down cases" is purposely omitted from the above enumeration; they have

their origin in dangers which can in no sense be called
obstructions or defects, and for which municipal corporations are not ordinarily responsible.

3. Injuries without remedy. Nor can it be useful to
more than call attention to the fact that many injuries
sustained on highways are and must be without remedy. In addition to the many accidents which happen
daily, and for which no one dreams of holding any one
responsible, four classes of cases may be mentioned
under this head : Thus,

(a) The exigencies of business and building, and the
pleasure, convenience and even safety of the public,
require more or less obstruction of the streets; and for
such reasonable and temporary obstruction, in absence of
negligence, there can be no liability.

"Necessity justifies many actions which would otherwise be nuisances. No one has the right to throw wood or
stones in the street at his pleasure ; nevertheless, as building is necessary, building materials may be laid therein
for a reasonable time and in a convenient manner. So
may a merchant occupy the street with his goods; in a
like manner may the common highways be temporarily
opened for the purpose of building vaults under them,
or, under like regulations, private drains may be connected with the common sewers or gutters, or houses and
other buildings with the streets, by alleys, door-steps and
the like. By such things as these, and many others,
which are justified by necessity or custom, may pub-

lic highways be occupied temporarily or permanently."

Smith v. Simmons, (Pa.) 29 A. L. J. 109.

Of a merchant, who, for the purpose of removing merchandise, placed a pair of skids across the side-walk to the steps of his store, the court say : "The defendant had the right to place the skids across the side-walk temporarily, for the purpose of removing the cases of merchandise. Every one doing business along a street in a populous city must have such a right, to be exercised in a reasonable manner, so as not to unnecessarily encumber and obstruct the side-walk."

Welsh r. Wilson, 101 N. Y. 254.

Though whether placing skids across a walk in a particular case is reasonable is for the jury to determine.

Jochem v. Robinson, (Wis.) 34 Alb. L. J. 456.

So it has been held in Georgia, that stretching ropes across a street during a firemen's parade, for the public safety and convenience, is a temporary and reasonable obstruction, for which a city would not be liable.

Simon v. Atlanta, (Ga.) 25 A. L. J. 477.

And in Maine, that blocks left a few hours in the street, for the purpose of repairing it, are of the same class.

Farrell v. Oldtown, 69 Me. 72.

And in New York, that a stepping-stone in front of a public building, for the accommodation of the public, is

allowable, and no liability is incurred for an injury caused
by it.

Dubois *v*. Kingston, 102 N. Y. 219.

(b) So also, in general, all injuries are remediless
which are caused by objects or obstructions not wrongfully or negligently made or continued, with knowledge
or notice of which those having a duty to make the highway safe cannot be charged.

(c) Those, also, to which the want of care of the person injured contributed in whole or in part.

(d) And those caused by the action of municipal corporations, in the exercise of their judicial or discretionary power ; for instance,

In the location and plan of streets, side-walks
and cross-walks,

Urquhart *v*. Ogdensburgh, 91 N. Y. 67.
Williams *v*. Grand Rapids, (Mich.) 53 Alb. L. J.
236.

Or location of street lamps.

Lyon *v*. Cambridge, 136 Mass. 419.

Some of the principles thus alluded to and decisions
cited, by way of illustration, may be considered more
fully hereafter.

CHAPTER II.

WHO MAY SUE.

A. **PERSON DIRECTLY INJURED.**
    1. Rule.
    2. Abatement.
B. **HUSBAND.**
    1. Rule.
    2. Abatement. Revival.
    3. Death of wife.
C. **PARENT.**
    1. Rule.
    2. Adopted child.
    3. Child's separate action.
D. **MASTER.**
E. **INJURIES RESULTING IN DEATH.**
    1. Generally.
    2. Outside New York.
F. **INJURIES RESULTING IN DEATH · NEW YORK.**
    1. Act of 1847.
    2. Amendment of 1849.
    3. Amendment of 1870.
    4. Code Civ. Pro.
    5. Relation of decedent to beneficiary.
    6. Existence of widow or next of kin.
    7. Fact of damage.
    8. Abatement.
    9. Extra-territorial effect.
    10. Common-law right of husband or parent.
    11. Bar by act of parent.
    12. Bar by act of decedent.
    13. Joinder of actions.

[In this, as well as other chapters, the principles stated and illustrated apply not only to the class of actions particularly under consideration, but to other similar actions.]

A. PERSON DIRECTLY INJURED.

1. Rule. *The person directly injured may of course seek his remedy in the courts.*

This is wholly independent of any cause of action which may accrue to any one whose interest is indirect.

A former judgment in favor of the wife is not, in an action by the husband, conclusive upon the question of negligence.

Neeson *v.* Troy, 29 Hun, 173.

2. Abatement. *The cause of action of the person directly injured does not survive to his personal representatives.*

Holton *v.* Daly, 106 Ill. 131 ; 27 Alb. L. J. 274.

Although it may be kept alive by prior stipulation.

Cox *v.* New York C. R. R. Co., 11 Hun, 621.

And does not abate after verdict, report or decision.

Code Civ. Pro. § 764.

B. HUSBAND.

1. Rule. *In case of personal injury to a married woman, her husband may maintain an action for care and attendance and loss of services and society.*

Cregin *v.* Brooklyn Crosstown R.R. Co., 83 N.Y. 595.
Jones *v.* Utica & B. R. R. R. Co., 40 Hun, 349.
Meigs *v.* Buffalo, 23 Week. Dig. 497.
Bowen *v.* Rome, Id. 406.

Groth *r.* Washburn, 34 Hun, 509.
Lynch *r.* Davis, 12 How. Pr. 323.
Philippi *v.* Wolff, 14 Abb. Pr. N. S. 196.
Hopkins *r.* Atlantic and St. L. R. R., 36 N. H. 9.
Lindsey *r.* Danville, 46 Vt. 144.
Stone *v.* Evans, 32 Minn. 243.

2. Abatement. Revival. *Though grounded in tort, the husband's action for injury to his wife abates on his death only as to the loss of society. As to the pecuniary loss, it may be revived in the name of the personal representatives, under 2 N. Y. Rev. St. 447.*

Cregin *r.* Brooklyn Crosstown R. R. Co., 83 N. Y. 595.

3. Death of wife. In case the wife die as the result of her injuries, there seems to be in New York some conflict of authority as to the husband's common-law right of action. This will be considered later. (See page 20.)

At any rate, the husband may maintain the action if his wife's death was not immediate, so that he was deprived of her society and assistance even for a brief period between the injury and her death.

Philippi *v.* Wolff, 14 Abb. Pr. N. S. 196.

C. PARENT.

1. Rule. *The father, or if he be not living, the mother, has an action for care and attendance and loss of services caused by the wrongful or negligent injury of a child.*

Traver *r.* Eighth Ave. R. R. Co., 4 Abb. Dec. 422.
Gilligan *r.* N. Y. and Harlem R. R. Co., 1 E. D. Smith, 453.

Whitaker v. Warren, 60 N. H. 20.
Pennsylvania R. R. Co. v. Kelly, 31 Penn. St. 372.
Faulkner v. Aurora, (Indiana) 27 Alb. L. J. 210.
Durkee v. Cent. Pac. R. R. Co., 56 Cal. 388.

2. Adopted child. In Whitaker v. Warren the child was that of the plaintiff only by adoption, and that not legal.

3. Child's separate action. In Traver v. Eighth Ave. R. R. Co., held, that the child might also recover for any expense and inability to work if it extended beyond his minority.

D. MASTER.

" It is a general principle that an action lies for an injury done to his slave, servant, apprentice, . . . in favor of the person who stands in place of a parent, by reason of which he has sustained a loss of service, or been put to expense in nursing or providing medicines."

Woodward v. Washburn, 3 Denio, 369, at p. 371.

This case was one for imprisonment of a hired servant. It is cited as authoritative in McMullen v. Hoyt, 2 Daly, at page 275. The rule, as above quoted, is comprehensive in its terms, and seems to be laid down as well-settled law.

E. INJURIES RESULTING IN DEATH.

1. Generally. *At common law, the right to maintain an action for personal injuries died with the person.*

Oldfield v. N. Y. & H. R. R. Co., 14 N. Y. 310, at p. 316.
Whitford v. Panama R. R. Co., 23 N. Y. 465, at p. 476.

In case the injuries result in death, there is in probably every State and jurisdiction a statutory cause of action accruing to some person or class of persons. These statutes differ in many particulars, but chiefly in prescribing who may bring the action; in some the right being giving to the personal representative for the benefit of specified persons, in others directly to the next of kin or other beneficiary.

2. Outside New York. No attempt will be made to examine or classify these different statutes. It may be noticed, however, by way of illustration, that in the following States the action must be brought by the personal representative, viz.: Massachusetts, Minnesota, Nebraska, Oregon. While in the following States the action accrues directly to the persons beneficially interested, viz.: California, Georgia, Illinois, Maryland, Missouri, Pennsylvania, Tennessee, Texas.

Under the statutes of different States the following adjudications may be of interest and use.

In Maryland, where the child has a cause of action for the death of the parent, held, that an adult child may recover.

  * B. & O. R. R. Co. v. State, 60 Md. 449.

Contra, in Georgia.

  Mott c. Central R. R. Co., 70 Ga. 680.

In Missouri, where minor children may sue within a year, held, that the child may sue within the year, though he have meantime become of age.

  Rutter v. Mo. Pac. Ry. Co., 81 Mo., 169.

In Tennessee, where the widow may sue for her children and herself, held, that she may discontinue the action against the objection of her children.

Greenlee r. Tenn., &c. R. R. Co., 5 Lea, 418.

In Texas, that a widow may sue, though she had lived separate from her husband.

Dallas, &c. R. R. Co. v. Spicker, 59 Tex. 435.

In Pennsylvania, where the parent may recover for the loss of a child, held, that the mother of an illegitimate child is not its *parent* within the statute.

Harkins v. Philadelphia & Reading R. R. Co., 15 Phila. 286.

In Massachusetts, in a case where a pregnant woman fell and was delivered of a child, which survived but a few minutes, held, that the child was not a *person*, so that an action would lie for its death.

Dietrich v. Northampton, 138 Mass. 14.

In Minnesota, where the action is by the representative, for the benefit of the widow and next of kin, held, that the complaint must allege the existence of a widow or next of kin.

Schwarz v. Judd, 28 Minn. 371.

F. INJURIES RESULTING IN DEATH; NEW YORK.

1. **Act of 1847.** The first enactment upon this subject is found in Session Laws of 1847, chapter 450, and reads as follows :

"§ 1. Whenever the death of a person shall be caused by wrongful act, neglect or default, and the act, neglect or default is such as would (if death had not ensued) have entitled the party injured to maintain an action and recover damages in respect thereof, then, and in every such case, the person who or the corporation which would have been liable if death had not ensued, shall be liable to an action for damages, notwithstanding the death of the person injured, and although the death shall have been caused under such circumstances as amount in law to felony.

"§ 2. Every such action shall be brought by and in the name of the personal representatives of such deceased person, and the amount recovered in every such action shall be for the exclusive benefit of the widow and next of kin of such deceased person, and shall be distributed to such widow and next of kin in the proportions provided by law in relation to the distribution of personal property left by persons dying intestate; and in every such action the jury may give such damages as they shall deem fair and just, with reference to the pecuniary injury resulting from such death, to the wife and next of kin of such deceased person; provided, that every such action shall be commenced within two years after the death of such deceased person.

"§ 3. This act shall take effect immediately."

2. **Amendment of 1849.** By chapter 256, Laws of 1849, this statute was amended in three important particulars:

First, so as to restrict the amount of damages to five thousand dollars.

Second, limiting the effect of the statute to suits and proceedings thereafter to be commenced.

Third, providing for the indictment and punishment of an agent or employee through whose wrongful act, neglect or default the death was caused.

3. Amendment of 1870. By chapter 78, Laws of 1870, two other important amendments were added:

First, adding the husband to the list of beneficiaries.

Second, providing that upon entry of judgment, interest be added to the amount of damages recovered, to be computed from the time of death.

It may be observed here, that prior to this amendment, it had been decided in several cases that the husband was not embraced within the description of next of kin of the wife, and was therefore entitled to no part of the recovery.

> Lucas *v.* New York C. R. R. Co., 21 Barb. 245.
> Dickens *v.* N. Y. Central R. R. Co , 23 N. Y. 158.
> Drake *v.* Gilmore, 52 N. Y. 389.

The last case was decided in 1873, but the cause of action had accrued prior to the amendment of 1870.

4. Code Civ. Pro. Sections 1902–1905 of the Code contain the present law upon the subject.

"§ 1902. The executor or administrator of a decedent, who has left him or her surviving, a husband, wife or next of kin, may maintain an action to recover damages for a

wrongful act, neglect or default, by which the decedent's
death was caused, against a natural person who, or a corporation which, would have been liable to an action in
favor of the decedent, by reason thereof, if death had not
ensued. Such an action must be commenced within two
years after the decedent's death.

"§ 1903. The damages recovered, in an action brought
as prescribed in the last section, are exclusively for the
benefit of the decedent's husband or wife, and next of
kin, and when they are collected they must be distributed by the plaintiff as if they were unbequeathed assets
left in his hands after payment of all debts and expenses
of administration. But the plaintiff may deduct therefrom the expenses of the action, and his commissions
upon the residue; which must be allowed by the surrogate, upon notice, given in such a manner and to such persons, as the surrogate deems proper.

"§ 1904. The damages awarded to the plaintiff may
be such a sum, not exceeding five thousand dollars, as the
jury, upon a writ of inquiry, or upon a trial, or where
issues of fact are tried without a jury, the court or the
referee, deems to be a fair and just compensation for the
pecuniary injuries resulting, from the decedent's death, to
the person or persons for whose benefit the action is
brought. When final judgment for the plaintiff is rendered, the clerk must add to the sum so awarded, interest thereupon from the decedent's death, and include it in
the judgment. The inquisition, verdict, report or decision may specify the day from which interest is to be computed; if it omits to do so, the day may be determined
by the clerk upon affidavits.

2

"§ 1905. The term 'next of kin,' as used in the fore-going sections, has the meaning specified in section 1870 of this act."

"§ 1870. The term 'next of kin,' as used in this title, includes all those entitled, under the provisions of of law relating to the distribution of personal property, to share in the unbequeathed assets of a decedent, after payment of debts and expenses, other than a surviving husband or wife."

It will be observed that the Code contains all the provisions of the old act as amended in 1870, except that for a criminal proceeding against the agent or employee, and contains nothing new except certain details and directions for practice.

Under this statutory provision, in its various forms, the following principles seem to have been settled by adjudication.

5. Relation of decedent to beneficiary. *The statute gives an action to the personal representatives, whenever the decedent, if living, might himself have maintained an action; the person killed need not have been a husband, father or protector.*

> Quin *v.* Moore, 15 N. Y. 432.
> Keller *v.* N. Y. C. R. R. Co., 7 How. Pr. 102.

"Although," the court says, in Quin *v.* Moore, "the legislature, in passing the act, were doubtless influenced by the evident justice of compelling the wrong-doer to compensate families dependent, in a greater or less degree, for support, on the life of the deceased."

6. Existence of widow, or next of kin. *Nor is it necessary to prove the existence of a widow or next of kin.*

> Oldfield r. N. Y. & Harlem R. R. Co., 14 N.Y. 310.
> Quin r. Moore, 15 N. Y. 432.
> Tilley r. Hudson River R. R. Co., 24 N. Y. 471.
> McMahon r. New York, 33 N. Y. 642.
> Dickens r. N. Y. C. R. R. Co., 28 Barb. 41.

7. Fact of damages. *Nor is it necessary to prove any pecuniary, or special damage.*

> Oldfield v. N. Y. & Harlem R. R. Co., 14 N. Y. 310.
> Keller v. N. Y. C. R. R. Co., 2 Abb. Dec. 480.

8. Abatement. *The action abates on the death of the wrongdoer, and cannot be revived against his personal representatives.* (Overruling Yertore v. Wiswall, 16 How. Pr. 8.)

> Hegerich r. Keddie, 99 N. Y. 258.

9. Extra-territorial effect. *The statute has no extra-territorial effect, so if the injury occurred in another State, there can be no action here, unless it appear that a statute similar to ours exists there.*

> Debevoise r. N. Y., L. E. & W. R. R. Co., 98 N. Y.
> 377.
> Mahler v. Norwich & N. Y. Trans. Co., 35 N. Y. 352.
> Beach r. Bay State Co., 10 Abb. Pr. 71; 30 Barb. 433.
> Whitford r. Panama R. R. Co., 23 N. Y. 465.
> McDonald r. Mallory, 7 Abb. N. C. 84; 77 N. Y. 546.
> Crowley r. Panama R. R. Co., 30 Barb. 99.
> Vandeventer r. N. Y. & N. H. R. R., 27 Barb. 244.

But may where it appears that the laws of that State are similar to those of this State, giving to the personal representatives a right of action in such cases ; it is not essential that the statute should be precisely the same.

Leonard v. Columbia Steam Nav. Co., 84 N. Y. 48.

10. Common-law right of husband or parent. Whether or not a father who has been deprived of the services of his child, or a husband who has lost the society and assistance of his wife, by acts of culpable negligence on the part of others, by means of which death has ensued, may not respectively maintain actions against the wrong-doer, to recover damages for such injury, is a question as to which the decisions are at variance ; one line of authorities holding that there is no cause of action but the statutory one in case of death, the other, that there is a common-law right of recovery.

(a.) In Ford *v.* Monroe, 20 Wend. 210, a child having been run over and killed, the father was held " entitled to recover such sum by way of damages as the services of the child would have been worth to him, until he became twenty-one years of age." This case was decided in 1838.

(b.) In Lynch *v.* Davis, 12 How. Pr. 323, Rensselaer special term, 1855, it was held that an action could not be sustained under the act of 1847 by a plaintiff, as *administrator* of the deceased wife, for injuries resulting from malpractice ; that the right of action vested in him as *husband.*

The court say : " The common-law gave the husband, and the father, a right to recover of the wrong-doer the pecuniary injury he had sustained by reason of the killing of his wife or child."

(c.) In Green v. Hudson R. R. R. Co., 28 Barb. 9, Oneida special term, 1858, affirmed at general term on same opinion, the opposite ground is taken, the court holding that no such action will lie, and supposing " the question has been too long settled in England and in this country to be disturbed, and that it would savor somewhat more of judicial knight-errantry than of legal prudence to attempt to unsettle what has been deemed at rest for more than two hundred and fifty years." Of Ford v. Monroe, the court say : " The case is certainly anomalous, sustained by no precedent, and in plain conflict with all previous authority."

(d.) In Whitford v. Panama R. R. Co., 23 N.Y. 465 (1861), this question was suggested, but the court say: " The present action does not in any way involve that controversy, and as the case just referred to (Green v. H R. R. R. Co.), is understood to be pending in this court on appeal, it is intended carefully to abstain from the expression of any opinion upon it."

(e.) In 1866 the Green case was affirmed by the court of appeals (2 Keyes, 294 ; 2 Abb. Dec. 277), the court paying its respects to both Ford v. Monroe and Lynch v. Davis. The particular point decided in the Green case was that a husband could not maintain an action for the instantaneous killing of his wife through the negligence of another. The same had been held in 1855, in Lucas v. N. Y. C. R. R. Co., 21 Barb. 245.

(f.) In McGovern v. N.Y. C. & H. R. R. R. Co., 67 N.Y. 417, decided in 1876, the court was expressly non-committal upon this point, which was not necessary to its decision, although the language of the opinion leads to the inference that its attention was not called to the Green case. The action was brought by a father as administrator of his minor son. The question arose upon an exception to the refusal of the trial judge to charge " that inasmuch as the father is entitled to the services of his son until he becomes of age, the earnings, which he might have made during his minority, are not to be considered." The court said : " Assuming, as seems to have been held in Ford *v.* Monroe, that a father can recover damages for the loss of service of his minor son, against a person who negligently caused his death, to be computed and ascertained from the time of his death, until the time when the son, if living, would have attained his majority, the question arises whether, in an action brought by the father, as administrator, under the statute, the entire damages may be recovered, including the loss of service, when, as in this case, the father elects to proceed for and claim his whole damages in the statutory action, and the recovery is for his exclusive benefit.

" We are inclined to the opinion that in such a case damages for the loss of service may be included in the recovery as a part of the pecuniary loss to the next of kin of the deceased, resulting from his death, and that a recovery will bar another action for the same damages by the father as such. . . .

" We confine our opinion to the precise case presented, assuming, on the authority of Ford *v.* Monroe, that the father has a right of action, independent of the statutes, for loss of service."

(g.) In Stuebing *v.* Marshall, 2 Civ. Pro. Rep. 77, N. Y. Common Pleas, General Term, the court carefully say :

" It is said that the father had a cause of action at common law, in addition to the cause of action created by the statute." But the point at issue was as to the effect of the father's release of all claims upon his cause of action as administrator, and the McGovern case is cited upon the precise point decided by it.

11. Bar by act of parent. *If the father be the sole beneficiary under the statute, a release by him will bar an action under the statute.*

Stuebing v. Marshall, 2 Civ. Pro. R. 77.

12. Bar by act of decedent. *If the wrong-doer settled with the deceased in his lifetime, and paid him the amount of his claim on account of the injury,* ([1]) *or if the decedent brought suit and recovered damages for the injury in his lifetime,* ([2]) *the personal representatives cannot maintain an action*

> ([1]) Dibble v. N. Y. & Erie Ry. Co., 25 Barb. 183.
> (Twice argued in Court of Appeals, but never decided. 21 How. Pr. 593 23 Id. 599.)
> ([2]) Littlewood v. New York, 89 N. Y. 24.
> (Overruling Schlichting v. Wintgen, 25 Hun, 626.)

The court in this case, speaking of the Dibble case, say : " The decision of the Supreme Court cannot, in the light of subsequent cases, be sustained on the ground that the representative suing under the statute merely succeeded to the right of action of the deceased, and was, for that reason, barred by his release. But on the ground that the statute was not intended to subject the defendant to an action, where he had made compensation to the deceased in his lifetime, and would not have been liable if the deceased had not died, I think the conclusion was correct."

13. Joinder of actions. *A person who is the administrator of the estates of two persons killed by the same accident, cannot join the two grievances in one action.*

Danaher *v.* Brooklyn, 4 Civ. Pro. R. 286.

CHAPTER III.

GROUNDS OF LIABILITY. WHOM TO SUE.

A. GROUNDS OF LIABILITY.
 First. Nuisance.
  1. Rule.
  2. Creator out of possession.
  3. Maintainer of nuisance.
  4. Knowledge.
  5. Ignorance as an excuse.
  6. Non-user as an excuse.
  7. License, generally.
  8. Effect of license.
  9. Degree of care under license.
 Second. Negligence.
  10. Negligent act.
  11. Neglect of duty.
B. WHOM TO SUE.
  1. Principal.
  2. Owner for fault of contractor.
  3. Officers.
  4. Agents and servants.
  5. Contractors.
  6. Abutting owners.
  7. Concurrent liability.

A. GROUNDS OF LIABILITY.

The liability for defects or obstructions in highways may be said to be grounded in either (1) nuisance, or (2) negligence. It should, perhaps, be added, that both of these may concur in a given case.

[25]

FIRST. NUISANCE.

1. Rule. *He who, without license or lawful authority, creates or maintains a dangerous obstruction in a public street, creates or maintains a nuisance, and is liable to persons injured thereby, irrespective of negligence or care.*

> Hart *v.* New York, 9 Wend. 571.
> Dygert *v.* Schenck, 23 Id. 446.
> Brown *v.* Cayuga & S. R. R. Co., 12 N. Y. 486.
> Congreve *v.* Smith, 18 N. Y. 79.
> Congreve *v.* Morgan, 18 N. Y. 84.
> Creed *v.* Hartmann, 29 N. Y. 591.
> Irvine *v.* Wood, 51 N. Y. 224.
> Baxter *v.* Warner, 6 Hun, 585.
> Clifford *v.* Dam, 81 N. Y. 52.
> Woram *v.* Noble, 41 Hun, 398.

2. Creator. The above rule is, however, subject to the following :

To charge one who has created a nuisance with liability for its continuance, after he has parted with the property upon which it is situated or caused, he must be shown to derive some benefit from the continuance, as by demising the premises and receiving rent ; or to have sold with warranty of the continued use of the property, as enjoyed while the nuisance existed, with covenants for the continuance of the nuisance.

> Hanse *v.* Cowing, 1 Lans. 288.
> People *v.* Livingston, 27 Hun, 105.

3. Maintainer. *A maintainer of a nuisance is a person deriving benefit from it, with knowledge of its existence. He may be the owner,* ([1]) *either occupying or receiving rent, or a tenant.* ([2])

> ([1]) Irvine *v.* Wood, 51 N. Y. 224.
> Anderson *v.* Dickie, 26 How. Pr. 105.

Walsh *v.* Mead. 8 Hun, 387.
Edwards *v.* N. Y. & H. R. R. Co., 98 N. Y. 245.
Swords *v.* Edgar, 59 N. Y. 28.
Davenport *v.* Ruckman, 37 N. Y. 568.
McGuire *v.* Spence, 91 N. Y. 303.
Congreve *v.* Smith, 18 N. Y. 79.
Congreve *v.* Morgan, Id. 84.

(2) Wasmer *v.* D., L. & W. R. R. Co., 80 N. Y. 212.
Swords *v.* Edgar, *supra.*
Irvine *v.* Wood, 51 N.Y. 224.
Edwards *v.* N. Y. & H. R. R. Co., *supra.*
Brown *v.* Cayuga & Susq. R. R. Co., 12 N.Y. 482.

In Swords *v.* Edgar the rule was laid down that where premises are affected by the nuisance at the time of the letting, the lessor is liable.

And in Walsh *v.* Mead, that this is so, even though the negligence of the tenant contributed to the injury.

This is subject to principles stated below, particularly the consideration of knowledge by the owner.

4. Knowledge. *He who knowingly maintains a nuisance is as responsible therefor as he who creates it.*

Davenport *v.* Ruckman, 37 N.Y. 568.
Wasmer *v.* D., L. & W. R. R. Co., 80 N. Y. 212.
Brown *v.* Cayuga & S. R. R. Co., 12 N. Y. 486.

(a) *Actual knowledge need not be proven; it may be implied from circumstances.*

Irvine *v.* Wood, *supra.*

"It was near their store, in plain view, and it was carelessness for them to occupy the store for months, and to use the hole, which, if not properly covered, was dangerous to travelers, and not examine into and know its condition. It was their duty to know its condition, and they must be held to the same responsibility as if they had actually known it."

5. **Ignorance.** *Actual ignorance of the nuisance may, under certain circumstances, relieve from liability.*

(a) Thus, where the owner did not create the nuisance, and purchased the premises subject to a lease, and the tenant was required to make all repairs, and the owner was ignorant of the defect, he was held not liable.

Woram *v.* Noble, 41 Hun, 398.

The court say : " To impose liability upon the defendant for the disaster that befell the plaintiff, would be to hold him responsible for the nuisance, when he had no agency in its creation, was without knowledge of its existence, derived no benefit from its continuance, and was destitute of authority for its abatement. Being innocent of everything but the ownership of the reversion at the time of the accident, no rule of justice requires a visitation of the consequences of the accident on the defendant, and nothing but a severe rule of law will justify a decision producing such a result. Our examination discloses no such rule."

It will be observed that the expression " derived no benefit from its continuance," as applied in this case, seems at variance with the usually recognized rule that the receiving of rent is a benefit so as to charge the landlord with the nuisance, provided he had knowledge of it.

Perhaps, however, it should be considered in connection with the principle laid down in Clancy *v.* Byrne, *infra*, where the court say : "If a landlord let premises, not in themselves a nuisance, and it is entirely at the option of the tenant to so use them or not that they shall not become so, *and the landlord will receive the same benefit if they be not so used*, the landlord is not responsible if, by the careless use by the tenant, they become a nuisance."

(b) So where the nuisance did not exist at the time of the letting, but arose from the manner in which the lessee used the premises, (¹) or was occasioned by the wrongful act of a stranger, (²) and the owner was unaware of the danger, he is not liable.

> (¹) Ryan *v.* Wilson, 87 N. Y. 471.
> Clancy *v.* Byrne, 56 N. Y. 129.
> (²) Wolf *v.* Kilpatrick, 101 N. Y. 146.

The first was the case of a building containing a revolving shaft, and the tenant placed a partition so near the shaft that it became dangerous to pass between, hence the injury.

In the case last cited, the injury was caused by the breaking by a stranger of a stone supporting the iron cover of a properly constructed coal-hole.

6. User. *Where a person acquires title to land upon which is a nuisance, the mere omission to abate or remove it does not render him liable ; actual use must be shown, or a request to abate.*

> Wenzlick *v.* McCotter, 87 N. Y. 122.

In that case, two houses had been built with a common leader from the two roofs, which was upon the defendant's house. The defendant purchased the house in that condition, and changed the conductors so that the water from that house no longer ran in the common leader, though the leader still remained on his house. The obstruction was ice, formed from water from the leader, coming, of course, from the roof of the adjacent house. The owner was held not liable.

7. License, generally. *The general rule as to nuisance (§ 1, above) is subject to the power usually given by charter to municipal corporations to make, or expressly or impliedly to license, temporary obstructions or excavations for the making and repairing of streets, the protection or convenience of the public, for laying pipes, for building, for the requirements of trade, for the convenient enjoyment of abutting buildings, or otherwise.*

> Rehberg v. New York, 91 N. Y. 137, 143.
> Nolan v. King, 97 N. Y. 565.
> See also cases cited in chap. I. § 3.

And such license may be implied from the knowledge of and absence of objection by the municipal authorities.

> Robbins v. Chicago, 4 Wall. 657.

8. Effects of license. *A license or permit from the proper authority changes the character of the liability from that for a nuisance to one for negligence or want of proper care.*

> Irvine v. Wood, 51 N. Y. 224.
> Wolf v. Kilpatrick, 101 N. Y. 146.
> Clifford v. Dam, 81 N. Y. 52.
> Mairs v. Manhattan Asn., 89 N. Y. 498.

Nolan *v.* King, 97 N. Y. 565.
Brusso *v.* Buffalo, 90 N. Y. 679.
McCamus *v.* Citizens' Gas-light Co., 40 Barb. 380.
Blake *v.* Ferris, 5 N.Y. 48.

In Irvine *v.* Wood, there was no license, but in the course of the opinion the court say : " Even if this hole was excavated in the street by permission of competent authority, the persons who originally excavated it were bound to do it in a careful manner, and to see that it was properly and carefully covered, so as not to be perilous to travelers upon the street. *They could get from the authorities no license for carelessness.* For in such case the city itself would be liable for the carelessness of its officers (Barton *v.* Syracuse, 36 N. Y. 54). And this liability attached not only to those who made the excavation, but to those who continued and used it in its improper and unsafe condition."

In Clifford *v.* Dam, it was proposed to prove a license which had not been pleaded. The court excluded the proposed evidence, and said : " If a permit was material, the effect of it would only be to mitigate the act from an absolute nuisance to an act requiring care in the construction and maintenance ; and to justify such a structure, it would be necessary not only to plead it, but also to allege and prove a compliance with its terms, and that the structure was properly made and maintained *to secure the same safety to the public that the sidewalk would have secured without it.* When permission is given by a municipal authority to interfere with a street solely for private use and convenience, and in no way connected with the public use, the person obtaining such permission must see to it that the street is restored to its original safety and usefulness."

9. Modification of above. The Court of Appeals have found it necessary in a late case to explain and somewhat modify the force of the expression above italicized, quoted from the opinion in Clifford *v.* Dam.

In Nolan *v.* King, 97 N. Y. 565, the obstruction consisted of a temporary bridge made over an excavation, for which a permit had been given. The trial justice charged to the full extent of the language of Clifford *v.* Dam, that "the defendant was under a liability to have the bridge constructed in such a manner that the plaintiff would not be subjected to any more personal risk than if the sidewalk had been there instead of the bridge." The Court of Appeals, commenting on this, say of the decision in Clifford *v.* Dam : "There a vault was built with an opening in the sidewalk to receive coal; but the cover to the opening, intended to remain there permanently, and to constitute a part of the sidewalk, was so imperfectly constructed that it gave way, and injury followed. We said that the builder was bound to make the sidewalk as safe as it was before excavated. But we did not say that he was bound to do that during the progress of construction. In the present case, the builder was required to restore the sidewalk which he had excavated to its original safe condition; but that is not saying he must keep it so during the progress of construction. That process implies and compels a temporary removal of the sidewalk, and either it must be left impassable, and guarded and protected as an excavation, or bridged above the sidewalk level so that the work of building or restoration can go on beneath it, and without obstruction to the public travel." And again : "In all such cases it is inevitable that the passage of the public, temporarily, is made less convenient and not so perfectly safe, as before the removal of the sidewalk; but if this is done with prudence and care, with good judgment, and properly and attentively, so as not to be perilous to passengers in the street, the builder is not responsible for an accident. The rule applied upon the trial of this case would tend to make impossible any temporary occupation of the street by builders during the process of construction."

SECOND. NEGLIGENCE.

The cases in which the liability is founded on negligence may be arranged in two classes: *first*, where the negligence is in the performance of an act; *second*, where it consists of the neglect of a duty.

1). **Negligent act.** *He who negligently creates or maintains an obstruction in a public street, is liable to persons injured thereby, irrespective of authority or license.*

> Sexton *v.* Zett, 56 Barb. 119. 44 N. Y. 430.
> Bliss *v.* Schaub, 48 Id 339.
> Steivermann *v.* White, 48 Super. 523.
> Dixon *v.* Brooklyn City & N. R. R. Co., 100 N. Y.
>   170. (See also cases cited under §§ 7, 8, *supra*.)
> Mairs *v.* Manhattan Real Estate Ass'n., 89 N. Y. 498.
> Robbins *v.* Chicago, 4 Wall. 657.
> Mulcairns *v.* Jaynesville, 34 Alb. L. J. 456.
> Indianapolis *v.* Emmelman, (Ind.) 35 Alb. L. J.
>   137.

The two cases last cited are examples of those in which a municipal corporation itself caused the obstruction.

3

11. Neglect of duty. *The person who, or corporation which, having imposed upon it the duty of keeping the streets safe for travel, is negligent in the performance of that duty, is liable to the person injured by a neglect, or omission, to properly perform such duty.*

> Bennett *v.* Whitney, 94 N. Y. 302.
> Hover *r.* Barkhoof, 44 N. Y. 113.
> Robinson *v.* Chamberlain, 34 N. Y. 389.
> Adsit *v.* Brady, 4 Hill, 630.

(Under this head come the liability of municipal corporations and of quasi-corporations and their officers.)

B. WHOM TO SUE.

1. Principal. *An individual, acting personally, or through agents or servants, or a corporation, is liable to a person suffering injury by a defect or obstruction created, maintained, or negligently suffered, as specified above.*

It is quite unnecessary to dwell upon or illustrate the liability of the principal, acting personally.

The liability of a principal for the act of his agent is also so elementary that it needs no attention.

2. Principal for fault of contractor. The application of the doctrine of *respondeat superior* to the case of a contractor and his principal may be considered more fully in another connection.

The liability of the principal is discussed in

> Blake *v.* Ferris, 5 N.Y. 48.
> Pack *v.* New York, 8 N.Y. 222.
> Kelly *v.* New York, 11 N.Y. 432.

and the absence of liability in

Baxter *v*. Warner, 6 Hun, 585.

3. Officers. *One who assumes the duties and is vested with the powers of a public officer is liable to an individual who sustains special damage by a neglect or omission to properly perform such duties.*

Bennett *v*. Whitney, 94 N. Y. 302.
Hover *v*. Barkhoof, 44 N. Y. 113.
Robinson *v*. Chamberlain, 34 N. Y. 389.
Adsit *v*. Brady, 4 Hill, 630.

In Adsit *v*. Brady the court say : " When an individual sustains an injury by the misfeasance or non-feasance of a public officer, who acts, or omits to act, contrary to his duty, the law gives redress to the injured party by an action adapted to the nature of the case."

This is denied in Weet *v*. Trustees of Brockport, 16 N. Y. 161, note, but the point was unnecessary to the decision of the case, and the opinion is disapproved in Robinson *v*. Chamberlain.

In Hover *v*. Barkhoof the court say : " The principle should be regarded as settled in this State, that public officers whose duties are not judicial, are answerable in damages to any one specially injured by their careless and negligent performance of or omission to perform, the duties of their office."

In Bennett *v*. Whitney the court add : " It was not a case of non-feasance, or omission to act at all, where in some cases it may be necessary to show adequate means in the hands of the officer; but a case of misfeasance, where the officer had acted, but conducted himself negligently, to the special injury of an individual."

4. **Agents and servants.** *It seems, also, that an agent (¹) or servant (²) is responsible for injuries resulting from negligence in his employment.*

(¹) Phelps *v.* Wait, 30 N. Y. 78.
(²) Wright *v.* Wilcox, 19 Wend. 343.
    Suydam *v.* Moore, 8 Barb. 358.
    Montfort *v.* Hughes, 3 E. D. Smith, 591.

But the mere architect or builder of a public work is answerable only to his *employer* for any want of care or skill in the execution thereof, and he is not liable to third persons for accidents or injuries which may occur after the completion of such work.

Albany *v.* Cunliff, 2 N.Y. 165.

5. **Contractor.** Under this head two classes arise :

(a) *A person entering into a contract with a city to keep its streets in repair, in effect contracts to perform that duty to the public in the place and stead of the municipality, and may be sued directly by the person injured.*

McMahon *v.* Second Ave. R. R. Co., 11 Hun, 347 ;
    75 N. Y. 231.

(b) *A contractor for the performance of certain work is liable for the negligence of himself and his subcontractors and employees in such performance.*

Creed *v.* Hartmann, 29 N. Y. 591.
Burns *v.* Dillon, 16 W. Dig. 368.
Finegan *v.* Moore, 46 N. J. L. 602.

(c) While a contractor is bound to put the street in safe condition, he is not bound to place a cross-walk where none had been before.

Thieme r. Gillen, 41 Hun, 443.

(d) A contractor may defend by showing that he acted by direction of city officers.

Cunningham v. Wright, 28 Hun, 178.

6. Lot-owner. *The abutting owner cannot, without special statute, be made liable, either directly or indirectly, for injuries occasioned by a defect in a sidewalk, not caused by him.*

Fulton r. Tucker, 5 T. & C. 621.
Moore v. Gadsden, 87 N. Y. 84.

So in Iowa.

Keokuk r. Independent District, 53 Iowa, 352.

Even where the charter provides that the city may compel lot-owners to repair, it cannot discharge its own liability by simply giving them notice.

Russell r. Canastota, 98 N. Y. 496.

7. Concurrent liability. *Two or more of the classes above named may be liable for the same defect or obstruction.* Thus:

(a) The owner and the tenant of premises on which a nuisance is maintained.

Davenport r. Ruckman, 37 N.Y. 568.
Irvine r. Wood, 51 N.Y. 224.
Jennings v. Van Schaick, 13 Daly, 510.

(b) The person causing the obstruction, and the city whose duty it is to care for the streets.

> Wilson *r.* Watertown, 5 T. & C. 579.
> Dixon *v.* Brooklyn City, &c. R. R. Co., 100 N. Y. 170.
> Trowbridge *v.* Forepaugh, 14 Minn. 133.

(c) To which list may be added the contractor with the municipal corporation to perform its duty in caring for the streets.

> McMahon *v.* Second Ave. R. R. Co., 75 N. Y. 231.

(d) The municipal corporation and the abutting owner, whom it may, by its charter, compel to repair and improve the sidewalk.

> Russell *v.* Canastota, 98 N.Y. 496.

(e) In all the cases above mentioned, where agents or servants are held to be liable to the person injured, it was also held that the principal or master would also be liable.

> Wright *v.* Wilcox, 19 Wend. 343.
> Suydam *v.* Moore, 8 Barb. 358.
> Phelps *v.* Wait, 30 N. Y. 78.

(f) For a personal injury occasioned by the negligence of several persons, there is both a separate and a joint liability.

> Cases cited under (a) and (e) above; also
> Creed *v.* Hartmann, 29 N. Y. 591.

In Minnesota it appears that the city and the person creating the obstruction cannot be sued jointly.

> Trowbridge *v.* Forepaugh, *supra.*

CHAPTER IV.

HIGHWAYS, HOW ESTABLISHED.

A. By Statutory Proceeding.
B. By Prescription.
    1. Introductory.
    2. In New York.
    3 In other States.
C. By Dedication.
    1. Introductory.
    2. Dedication defined.
    3. Intent must be proven.
    4. Manner of proof.
    5. Intent shown by acts.
    6. Conveyance by map, binding on parties.
    7. Contra, as to the public.
    8. Right of way.
    9. Map, by whom made.
    10. Actual map.
    11. Inference from user.
    12. Revocation.
    13. Acceptance, generally.
    14. How proven.
    15. Acts to prove.
    16. User.
    17. Adjudications as to user.
    18. Statutory acceptance by limitation.
    19. Leading cases.
    20. Miscellaneous cases.

In order to establish a liability for injuries received, upon the ground that they were received upon a public

[39]

highway, it is many times necessary to prove the existence of the highway as a public thoroughfare.

There a.e, speaking generally, three ways by which streets may be established :

First. By statutory proceeding.
Second. By prescription.
Third. By dedication and acceptance.

The liability of the person or corporation at fault is, however, wholly independent of the way by which the street became such.

Phelps *v.* Monkato, 23 Minn. 276.
Beaudean *v.* Cape Girardeau, 71 Mo. 392.

A. BY STATUTORY PROCEEDING.

There are in every State statutes providing for the establishment of highways, and for their alteration and discontinuance.

Some of these acts are of general application throughout the State,—as chapter 16 of the Revised Statutes of the State of New York ; others are special, contained in the charters of, or otherwise pertaining to particular municipal corporations.

It is sufficient, without going into the details of these statutes, to notice that they, in general, authorize certain designated officers (in New York called commissioners of highways, under the State law), to lay out and alter roads or streets, and they provide for the condemnation of the required land, and compensation to the owners.

In the charters of municipal corporations it is customary to provide that all existing streets and highways shall be public highways.

And, in such a case, the question whether or not they are highways, is at rest, save to inquire, as matter of fact, whether given streets come within that statute.

Hickok v. Plattsburgh, 41 Barb. 130.

In determining that question, a provision of the charter relieving the city of the control of a portion of it, does not detract from the character of any part of it in actual public use as a highway.

Baxter v. Warner, 6 Hun, 585.

B. By Prescription.

1. In some States statutes exist, prescribing a length of uninterrupted user of roads which shall give rise to the presumption that the same are public highways, and shall constitute them such. In other States it is held that the period of the statute of limitations in real property actions is applicable for that purpose.

2. In New York, it is provided, in the general highway law, that "all roads not recorded, which have been, or shall have been, used as public highways for twenty years or more, shall be deemed public highways." The same act also provides that all highways that have ceased to be traveled, or used as such for six years, shall cease to be highways for any purpose.

2 R. S. 7th ed. p. 1249, §§ 99, 100.

" Formerly, the user must have been twenty years
previous to and next preceding March 21, 1797 (1
R. L. 1801, p. 595 ; 2 R. L. 1813, 277, § 24) ; and this
[supreme] court seems to have considered itself bound
to allow no claim founded on user for any other term
(Galatian v. Gardner, 7 Johns. 106 ; People v. Lawson,
17 Id. 277). But twenty years' general occupation was
allowed by the act of February 21, 1817 (Laws of 1817,
p. 32, § 3)."

Pearsall v. Post, 20 Wend. 111, at p. 116.

Under this act it was decided in Devenpeck v. Lam-
bert, 44 Barb. 596, that an uninterrupted user for more
than twenty years constitutes a street by prescription,
notwithstanding :

(1) The several owners of the land did not so intend ;
(2) The owner be a lunatic, an infant, or a married
woman ;
(3) And had no knowledge of the user during the
entire term.

Also that declarations of an owner that he did not
intend dedication, would not take the place of actual
interruption of user.

In Re Rebuilding Bridge, &c., 100 N. Y. 642, the
question was suggested whether mere user by the public
for twenty years, without any action of the town authorities in laying out, or recording or improving or accepting
the road, would make a highway. But the question was
unnecessary to the decision of the case, and was not discussed.

In Cole *v.* Van Keuren, 6 T. & C. 480 ; 64 N. Y. 646, held, that the record of a highway under the general highway act is not conclusive, upon the question of prescription, upon the owner of the soil, claiming it as a private road.

3. In other States. (a) In MASSACHUSETTS, it has been held that if for more than twenty years there has been a constant and uninterrupted use of a sidewalk by the public, under a claim of right to use it as part of a public street, the city is liable for a defect in it.

Veale *v.* Boston, 135 Mass. 187.

(b) In IOWA, that to establish a highway by prescription, there must have been a general, uninterrupted use by the public, under a claim of right, for ten years, being the period prescribed by the statute of limitations.

State *v.* Tucker, 36 Iowa, 485.
State *v.* Green, 41 Iowa, 693.

(c) In INDIANA, that a road becomes a public highway by twenty years' user, or in less time with the assent of the owner, and such use that public and private interests would be affected by a change.

Ross *v.* Thompson, 78 Ind. 90.

(d) In ILLINOIS, that a street thrown open for public use, and used by the public over twenty years, becomes a highway.

Chicago *v.* Wright, 69 Ill. 318.

Also, that a tract of land used for a public road, and traveled generally by the public as such, without objec- ·

tion by the owner, for more than twenty years, though not fenced on either side, may become a highway by prescription.

Slingart v. Holliday, 2 Ill. Ap. 45.

(e) In NORTH CAROLINA, the period is twenty years. But mere use of a foot-path or neighborhood road for twenty years, will not constitute a dedication.

Boyden v. Achenbach, 74 N. C. 539.

(g) In MINNESOTA, the period is fixed by statute at six years.

Minn. Gen. St. 1878, ch. 13, § 47.

This statute held to be purely prospective, in

State v. Waholz, 28 Minn. 114.

Certain special provisions, fixing a short limitation in various municipal corporations in New York, are merely in aid of establishing dedication or acceptance of streets, and will be considered in that connection.

C. BY DEDICATION.

1. **Dedication and acceptance.** *The third method of establishing highways, and the one which has given rise to far the greater part of the adjudication upon the subject, involves two elements: First, a dedication by the owner of the fee or by some one having the right to dedicate; and second, an acceptance by the public.*

Niagara Falls Suspension Bridge Co. v. Bachman,
66 N. Y. 261.

Chicago *r.* Thompson, 9 Ill. Ap. 524.
Browne *r.* Bowdoinham, 71 Me. 144.

This is an elementary principle, and is laid down or implied in all the cases cited below.

Dedication defined. "Dedication, as the term is used with reference to this subject, is the act of devoting or giving property for some proper object, and in such manner as to conclude the owner."

Hunter *v.* Trustees of Sandy Hill, 6 Hill 407, at p. 411.

"An act by which the owner of the fee gives to the public, for some proper object, an easement in his lands."

Curtis *r.* Keesler, 14 Barb. 511, at p. 521.

3. Necessity of proof. *The intent to dedicate must be clearly manifested.*

Grinnell *r.* Kirtland, 2 Abb. N. C. 386 ; S. C., 6 Daly, 356 ; S. C., aff'd, without opinion, 68 N. Y. 629.
McMannis *r.* Butler, 51 Barb. 436.
Holdane *r.* Cold Spring, 21 N. Y. 474.
Niagara Falls, &c. Bridge Co. *r.* Bachman, 66 N.Y. 261.
Flack *r.* Green Island, 23 W. Dig. 534.
Pierpoint *r.* Harrisville, 9 W. Va. 215.
State *r.* Tucker, 36 Iowa, 485.
Sullivan *r.* State, 52 Ind. 309.
•Chicago *r.* Thompson, 9 Ill. Ap. 524.
Porter *r.* Attica, 33 Hun. 605.
People *r.* Blake, 60 Cal. 497.
Wiggins *r.* Tallmadge, 11 Barb. 457.
Carpenter *r.* Gwynn, 35 Barb. 395.

4. Manner of proof. While, of course, a direct conveyance of land or an easement in land for a highway to the public authorities would constitute a dedication, that is not essential or at all usual.

No deed or other writing is necessary to constitute dedication.

> Cook *v*. Harris, 61 N. Y. 448.
> Hunter *v*. Sandy Hill, 6 Hill, 407.
> Curtis *v*. Keesler, 14 Barb. 511, at p. 521.

5. Intent. Shown by acts. *Dedication may be established by any evidence which shows the intent of the owner to dedicate. The intent may be inferred from acts and declarations of the owner.*

> Sheen *v*. Slothart, 29 La. An. 630.
> Brakken *v*. Minneapolis, &c. Ry. Co., 29 Minn. 41.
> People *v*. Blake, 60 Cal. 497.
> Cook *v*. Harris, 61 N. Y. 448.
> Re Cooper, 6 W. Dig. 144.
> McMannis *v*. Butler, 51 Barb. 436.
> Wiggins *v*. Tallmadge, 11 Barb. 457.
> Denning *v*. Roome, 6 Wend. 651.

In Wiggins *v*. Tallmadge, the act of dedication consisted in the opening of a lane or road by two owners upon their boundary line, to accommodate the adjoining lands.

In Re Cooper, it consisted in grading, paving and guttering, and in Denning *v*. Roome the former owner paid an assessment for paving.

6. Conveyance by map. *A conveyance of lots with reference to a map, on which the land is laid off in streets and* *squares, whether the map is made and filed by the owner* [1] *or is a public map,* [2] *is, as to the owner, a dedication of the streets, alleys and squares referred to, to the extent and as designated on the map.*

[1] Dewitt *v.* Ithaca, 15 Hun, 568.
McMannis *v.* Butler, 51 Barb 436.
Bridges *v.* Wyckoff, 67 N. Y. 130.
Taylor *v.* Hopper, 2 Hun, 646 ; 62 N. Y. 649.
Child *v.* Chappell, 9 N. Y. 246, at p. 257.
Post *v.* Pearsall, 22 Wend. 425.
(See many cases cited at p. 435.)
Cox *v.* James, 45 N. Y. 557.
Baton Rouge *v.* Bird, 21 La. An. 244.
Bartlett *v.* Bangor, 67 Maine, 460.
[2] Re Ingraham, 4 Hun, 495. 64 N. Y. 310.
Clark *v.* Elizabeth, 40 N. J. L. 172.
Re Thirty-ninth Street, 1 Hill, 191.
Bissell *v.* N. Y. C. R. R. Co., 23 N. Y. 61.
People *v.* Lambier, 5 Denio, 9.
People *v* Lochfelm, 102 N. Y. 1.
Also cases cited next below.

7. Contra. *But as to the public, it is but an offer to dedicate, and is not complete until accepted by competent authority, or by user.*

Dewitt *v.* Ithaca, 15 Hun, 568.
Oswego *v.* Oswego Canal Co., 6 N. Y. 257.
Underwood *v.* Stuyvesant, 19 Johns. 181.
Wohler *v.* Buffalo & State Line R. R. Co., 46 N.Y. 686.
Niagara Falls, &c. Br. Co. *v.* Bachman, 66 N.Y. 261.
Taylor *v.* Hopper, 62 N. Y. 649.
Re Ingraham, 4 Hun, 495.
Strong *v.* Brooklyn, 68 N. Y. 1.
Child *v.* Chappell, 9 N. Y. 246.

8. Right of way. *And as to the owner it is only good as a right of way, until accepted.*

Badeau *v.* Mead, 14 Barb. 328.
Taylor *v.* Hopper, 62 N.Y. 649.

Holdane *v.* Cold Spring, 21 N. Y. 474.
Fonda *v.* Borst, 2 Abb. Dec. 155 ; 2 Keyes, 48.
Grinnell *v.* Kirtland, 2 Abb. N. C. 386.

In Badeau *v.* Mead,—a case arising in the country,— it was assumed that the rule would be different as to city lands.

In Grinnell *v.* Kirtland, however, it is expressly held to apply as well to urban as to rural property.

9. Map, by whom made. *The map must have been made or accepted by the owner of the premises, or by some one having the right to dedicate the land.*

Re Rhinelander, 68 N. Y. 105.

In this case, it was held that where the map was made by the municipal authorities, and the owners had nothing to do with it, the mere fact that the land on each side of the street was afterwards divided into lots, is without significance.

In People *v.* Brooklyn, 48 Barb. 211, the map was made and filed by commissioners in a partition suit, upon actual partition of the land among tenants in common. All subsequent conveyances carried to the centre of the streets ; one of them describing the land within the street as subject to the public use as a highway. Held, that the original map and partition was a dedication, and that the subsequent sales must be interpreted as conveying as and for the purposes of public streets.

In Flack *v.* Green Island, 23 W. Dig. 534, held, that a map made by a civil engineer, and recognized for years by the owners and the public authorities, and adopted by unmistakable acts, is equally conclusive for all purposes of a dedication as if made by the land-owners, or by their direction.

10. Actual map. *To constitute a dedication, the deed must refer to a street or avenue actually laid out on maps actually made and filed.*

Re Eleventh Avenue, 49 How. Pr. 208. 81 N. Y. 433.

11. Inference from user. There seems to be a line of authorities holding that, aside from prescription, dedication by the owner may be inferred from uninterrupted user for a great length of time; or, at least, that user may be an element in determining the intent of the owner. Among such cases are:

> Denning *v.* Roome, 6 Wend. 651.
> Curtis *v.* Keesler, 14 Barb. 511.
> Hunter *v.* Sandy Hill, 6 Hill, 407.
> Wilson *v.* Sexon, 27 Iowa, 15.
> Daniels *v.* Chicago, &c. R. R. Co., 35 Iowa, 129.
> Sullivan *v.* State, 52 Ind. 309.

12. Revocation. *Dedication may be revoked by the owner at any time before acceptance, whether by express corporate or official act, or user,* ([1]) *but not after.* ([2])

> Bridges *v.* Wyckoff, 67 N. Y. 130.
> Lee *v.* Sandy Hill, 40 N. Y. 442.

Quære as to ([1]),

> Jordan *v.* Otis, 37 Barb. 50.

4

Contra as to (^{1}),

> M. E. Church *v.* Hoboken, 33 N. J. L. 13.

Contra as to (^{2}),

> Adams *v.* Saratoga, &c. R. R. Co., 11 Barb. 414.
> Rev'd on other grounds, 10 N. Y. 328.
> Cook *v.* Harris, 61 N. Y. 448.

(a) Revocation can be made by no one who has not succeeded to the title of the original proprietors.

> McMannis *v.* Butler, 51 Barb. 436.

(b) Whether the revocation is made by putting a building partly across the street, is a question for the jury.

> Id.

13. Acceptance, generally. *Dedication of land or an easement, by the owner of the fee, is not enough to constitute a highway. This must be supplemented by an acceptance of the same, either express or implied.*

> See cases cited under (7) above ; also, next section.
> Corwin *v.* Corwin, 24 Hun, 147.
> Rozell *v.* Andrews, 103 N. Y. 150.

14. How proven. *Acceptance must be clearly proven, either by formal action or by distinct and unequivocal circumstances.*

> McMannis *v.* Butler, 51 Barb. 436.
> Holdane *v.* Cold Spring, 21 N. Y. 474.
> Niagara Falls, &c. Bridge Co. *v.* Bachman, 66
>   N. Y. 261.
> Grinnell *v.* Kirtland, 2 Abb. N. C. 386.
> Byrne *v.* N. Y. C. & H. R. R. R. Co., 94 N. Y. 12.
> Fonda *v.* Borst, 2 Abb. Dec. 155.
> Clements *v.* West Troy, 16 Barb. 251.

Jordan r. Otis, 37 Barb. 50.
Oswego r. Oswego Canal Co., 6 N. Y. 257.
Bissell r. N. Y. C. R. R Co., 23 N. Y. 61.
Booraem r. No. Hudson Ry. Co., 39 N. J. Eq. 465.
Ex parte Pittsburgh Alley, 104 Pa. St. 622.
Manderschid r. Dubuque, 29 Iowa, 73.
State r. Tucker, 36 Iowa, 485.
Forbes r. Balenseifer, 74 Ill. 183.
Flack r. Green Island, 23 W. Dig. 534.

15. Acts to prove. *It may be proven by acts of the munici-pality or its officers.*

Cook r. Harris, 61 N. Y. 448.
Hillier v. Sharon Spr., 28 Hun, 344.
Sewell r. Cohoes, 75 N. Y. 45.
Niven r. Rochester, 76 N. Y. 619.
Schomer r. Rochester, 15 Abb. N. C. 57.
Tierney v. Troy, 41 Hun, 120.
People r. Loehfelm, 102 N. Y. 1.
Pomfrey r. Saratoga Springs, 104 N. Y. 459.
And many other cases.

Among the acts may be mentioned a few, as :

(a) Resolution to enter street in records.

Re Cooper, 6 W. Dig. 144.

(b) Taking charge of, regulating, paving and repair-ing.

Sewell v. Cohoes, *supra*.
McMannis v. Butler, 51 Barb. 436.
Shartle v. Minneapolis, 17 Minn. 308.

Laying gas and water pipes, and lighting street.

Re Ingraham, 4 Hun, 495.
Modified, on other grounds, 64 N. Y. 310.

(c) Resolutions of common council as to same.

Same cases ; also,
Schomer r. Rochester, 15 Abb. N. C. 57.
Niven v. Rochester, 76 N. Y. 619.

16. User. *Acceptance may be proven by user, with other evidence.*

> Curtis *v.* Keesler, 14 Barb. 511.
> Pomfrey *v.* Saratoga, 34 Hun, 607 ; 104 N. Y. 459.
> Sewell *v.* Cohoes, 75 N. Y. 45.
> People *v.* Blake, 60 Cal. 497.
> Brakken *v.* Minneapolis, &c. Ry. Co., 29 Minn. 41.
> Dewitt *v.* Ithaca, 15 Hun, 568.
> Kennedy *v.* Le Van, 23 Minn. 513.
> Manderschid *v.* Dubuque, 29 Iowa, 73.
> Forbes *v.* Balenscifer, 74 Ill. 183.
> Flack *v.* Green Island, 23 W. Dig. 534.
> People *v.* Lochfelm, 102 N. Y. 1.
> Driggs *v.* Phillips, 103 N. Y. 77.

17. Adjudications as to user. The effect of user is usually considered in cases involving its effect upon both dedication and acceptance. For that reason it has been thought best to examine a few of such cases in this dual capacity.

(a) To constitute dedication by user, no particular time is necessary. If express and unequivocal, a short time is enough.

> Carpenter *v.* Gwynn, 35 Barb. 395.
> Clements *v.* West Troy, 10 How. Pr. 179.
> Curtis *v.* Keesler, 14 Barb. 511.
> Hunter *v.* Sandy Hill, 6 Hill, 407.
> Child *v.* Chappell, 9 N. Y. 246.
> Cook *v.* Harris, 61 N. Y. 448.
> McMannis *v.* Butler, 51 Barb. 448.
> Denning *v.* Roome, 6 Wend. 651.
> Hiner *v.* Jeanpert, 65 Ill. 428.
> Ogle *v.* Phila., &c. R. R. Co., 3 Houst. (Del.) 267.

In Denning *v.* Roome, it is stated that the length of time to constitute dedication is not settled, "probably because the presumption does not depend on that alone."

(b) It should be for such a length of time that the public accommodation and private rights might be materially affected by an interruption of the enjoyment.

Cincinnati v. White, 6 Peters, 431.
McMannis v. Butler, 51 Barb. 436.

(c) User even for more than twenty years against the will of the owner cannot be urged by the public as the foundation of prescription or evidence of dedication.

Pearsall v. Post, 20 Wend. 111 ; 22 Wend. 425.
Pearsall v. Hewitt, 20 Wend. 111 ; 22 Wend. 559.
Sullivan v. State, 52 Ind. 309.

(d) "It is to be borne in mind that mere user is not sufficient; though user may be taken in connection with other evidence to prove actual dedication. To show that persons have exercised the right for a series of years, is but a link in the chain of proof to establish the conclusion that the owner of the fee has appropriated or set apart and given to the public an easement or use in his land, which he cannot recall at pleasure."

Curtis v. Keesler, 14 Barb. 523.

(e) User *alone*, to constitute dedication, must have continued twenty years.

Gould v. Glass, 19 Barb. 179.

And then the importance of dedication disappears, since the statute makes the highway by prescription.

Porter v. Attica, 33 Hun, 605.

(f) In People *v*. Livingston, 27 Hun, 105, the question of user as establishing dedication was considered.

"Fifty years ago, the owner of the lot told some of his neighbors that if they would help him build a stone-wall from the main road to the lake, they could drive their sheep to the lake and wash them there. They helped him build the wall, and since then, these persons and their successors, as they had occasion, drove their sheep across this lot, which adjoined the Knox road on one side and the lake on the other, to an enclosure upon the lake shore, and there washed them. As this lot was un-fenced along the Knox road, the public, in passing to and from the lake, crossed it where it was most convenient. Picnic parties, fishermen and others crossed over it to and from the lake. In the winter, ice was drawn from the lake across it, and sometimes when the lake was frozen teams were driven across it to and from the lake. There is no regular travelled road across the lot, and the evidence is that when people crossed it, they crossed it in different places. The sheep, it is true, made a beaten path from the Knox road to the sheep pen, but there does not appear to have been any other well-defined path. All over the lot were wagon and cattle tracks, and the evidence fails to show that the travel, except by the sheep, was in an uniform route, and except that on the shore of the lake, the tracks were more united. . . . . The license given by the owner of the land to those who helped him build his stone-wall, to drive their sheep across his lot, conferred no rights upon the public. . . Leaving the sheep path out of the case, and no road across the lot ever existed, unless the whole lot should be condemned for that purpose. . . . If all the travel across the lot for the last twenty years had been confined to one route, it is not improbable that a highway by user would have been located and established; but the burden was upon the people to prove a highway over the route they described, and this they utterly failed to do."

(g) In McMannis v. Butler, 51 Barb. 436, a map had been made and filed by the proprietors in 1827, showing the road, which was in continuous public use from 1832 to 1865. Held, accepted by public user. It also appeared in the case that the street had been accepted by acts of the common council.

The rule of dedication and acceptance by user is laid down in that case, as follows:

Clear, unequivocal and decisive acts of the owners, amounting to an explicit manifestation of their will to make a permanent abandonment and dedication of the land, is sufficient to establish dedication.

If land dedicated is, without any intermediate period, unequivocally used and occupied for any continuous period of time by the public at large, it amounts to an adoption of the dedication.

(h) In Wiggins v. Tallmadge, 11 Barb. 457, the owners opened a road to accommodate adjacent lands.

It was used forty years by the public; and, more than twenty years after, the authorities had connected it with a public road beyond. Held, dedication and acceptance.

18. Statutory acceptance by limitation. In many municipalities in New York, there is a statute of which the
Rochester act (Laws of 1880, chap. 14, section 163) is an
example:

" Whenever any street, alley or lane shall have been
opened to or used by the public for the period of five
years, the same shall thereby become a street, alley or
lane for all purposes, and the said common council and
executive shall have the same authority and jurisdiction
over and right and interest in the same as they have by
law over the other streets, alleys, lanes and highways,
laid out over it."

Under this act, held that no formal act of acceptance,
other than the acceptance of the charter containing such
section, was needed.

Requa v. Rochester, 45 N. Y. 129.

Also, that it was not intended to have a retroactive
effect, so as to divest parties of existing rights.

McMannis v. Butler, 49 Barb. 177. (Reversed, 51
Barb. 436, on other grounds.)

Under the Brooklyn act it was held in Baldwin v.
Jenkins, 1 W. Dig. 398, Brooklyn city court, general
term, that mere throwing open and use would not have
the effect of dedication, unless accepted by the authorities.

This, however, would seem questionable, in view of
the following rule:

Such statutes take the place of an acceptance, and that only. The intention of the owner to dedicate must still be proven.

> Strong *v.* Brooklyn, 68 N. Y. 1.
> Morse *v.* Troy, 38 Hun, 301.

In the latter case, the accident happened May 1, 1877.

The land had been deeded in 1871, with a proviso that a street should be opened on or before June 1, 1872. Held, that five years not having elapsed, there was no dedication or " throwing open " by the deed.

Also that, although the owner had done some working and grading, it was not sufficient (as was necessary) to enable the city to have accepted the dedication at the beginning of the five years period, or at any time within it.

19. Some leading cases. It may be useful to notice a few adjudications upon the subject of dedication and acceptance of streets, as applied in considering the liability of municipal corporations for failure to keep the streets in safe condition for travel.

(a) In Sewell *v.* Cohoes, 11 Hun, 626 ; 75 N. Y. 45, the *locus in quo* was a strip of land along the Erie canal, upon State land, but which the city had caused to be paved and graded, and it was used as a public street.

This was crossed by a bridge so low that the plaintiff —the driver of a circus wagon—was struck by the bridge and injured.

Held, that the city, by its action, in taking charge of,

regulating and grading, was estopped from denying that
the place was a public highway.

Also, that it was competent to prove resolutions of
the common council as to grading and paving.

And resolutions after the accident, directing the
removal of the bridge, to show that the city exercised
control.

(b) In Hiller *v.* Sharon Springs, 28 Hun, 344, held,
that though an individual cannot, by putting a sidewalk
along his premises, compel the authorities to accept it:
yet, where he does so construct one, not merely for his
private benefit, the authorities may, by their acquiescence and other acts, show their acceptance, and thus
bind themselves to keep the sidewalk in repair.

That no distinct act of adoption or acceptance need
be shown, nor any positive recognition of it.

(c) In Porter *v.* Attica, 33 Hun, 605, the defective
sidewalk was at the intersection of a street with a way
leading to several dwellings; the way had been there
forty years, and the houses twenty or more.

Upon a change of grade of the sidewalk on the street,
that of the way had not been changed; but the authorities had provided an earth approach to it. This washed
away, and the hole thus formed caused the injury.

Held, for the jury to say whether it had become a
highway, so that the village were bound to repair it, both
as to user and dedication and acceptance.

(The opinion in this case contains a useful examination of authorities showing different rulings upon the question of user as constituting acceptance.)

(d) In Pomfrey *v.* Saratoga Springs, 34 Hun, 607, the injury was caused by snow falling from a roof upon a sidewalk in a village.

It was part of a continuous street; had been so used for many years; the city had put a sidewalk upon part of the street.

The owner used the space in question to cross to his barn, and left and washed carriages there; the public used it as a sidewalk. There had been no formal acceptance.

Held, that the jury were justified in finding dedication and acceptance.

This case was distinguished in Veeder *v.* Little Falls, 100 N. Y. 343, upon the ground that the dangerous embankment there was on State land, where the village had wrongfully placed a street, and where they had no right to put a railing.

20. Miscellaneous adjudications.

(a) The highway act of 1813, stating that if a road is not opened or worked within six years from the time of laying out, it shall cease to be a highway, does not refer to those *dedicated* to public use.

McMannis *v.* Butler, 51 Barb. 436.

(b) Dedication as a private way, or any length of user as such, is not enough.

State v. Tucker, 36 Iowa, 485.

(c) Dedication may be established, although proven as to only part of the highway.

     Havana v. Biggs, 58 Ill. 483.

(d) So, though there be no outlet, or the street end in a private way.

     Saunders r. Townsend, 26 Hun, 308.
     Wiggins v. Tallmadge, 11 Barb. 457.
     People v. Kingman, 24 N. Y. 559.
     People v. Van Alstyne, 3 Abb. Dec. 575.
     See discussion, Hickok v. Plattsburgh, 41 Barb.
     130.

(e) Or though it be only a public foot-way.

     Tyler v. Sturdy, 108 Mass. 196.

(A list of useful authorities on dedication is found at 2 Abb. N. C. 400, note.)

CHAPTER V.

1. Introductory. Having thus far noticed certain incidental and preliminary subjects, we come to the principal topic,—the liability of municipal corporations to respond in damages to persons injured by unsafe streets.

2. General rule. The general principle of such liability is nowhere better stated than in the case first below cited, as follows:

Municipal corporations proper, having the powers ordinarily conferred upon them respecting streets within their limits, owe to the public the duty to keep them in a safe condition for use in the usual mode by travellers, and are liable in a civil action for special injury resulting from neglect to perform this duty.

Ehrgott *v*. New York, 96 N.Y. 264, at p. 271.

Citing

New York *v*. Furze, 3 Hill, 612.
Conrad *v*. Ithaca, 16 N. Y. 158.
Requa *v*. Rochester, 45 N. Y. 129.
Barnes *v*. District of Col., 91 U. S. 540.
Hutson *v*. New York, 9 N. Y. 163.
Davenport *v*. Ruckman, 37 N. Y. 568.
Hume *v*. New York, 74 N. Y. 264.

[61]

And cited in

> Hunt *v*. New York, 52 Super. 198.

See also,

> Reinhard *v*. New York, 2 Daly, 243.
> Gorham *v*. Cooperstown, 59 N. Y. 660.
> Knoxville *v*. Bell, (Tenn.) 12 Lea, 157.
> Griffin *v*. Williamstown, 6 W. Va. 312.

And other cases cited in chap. VII. § 1, *post.*

And this is true by night as well as by day.

> Davenport *v*. Ruckman, *supra.*
> Rome *v*. Dodd, 58 Ga. 238.

3. Occasions. And the occasions of such liability are well expressed in Atchison *v.* King, 9 Kansas, 550, as follows :

(1) Negligent construction of street by city.
(2) Causing defects therein after they are made.
(3) Negligently permitting defects to continue.

Or, as stated in Gorham *v.* Cooperstown, 59 N.Y. 660 : "Municipal corporations are not guarantors for the absolute safety of all persons from injury by reason of defects in or obstructions of the streets or highways of the municipality. They are only liable when the defects or obstructions are the results of their acts, or of some neglect or omission of duty by them or their servants or agents ; and individuals in the use of streets receive injuries therefrom without fault on their part ; some overt act of the municipality or its officers, resulting in injury to third persons, or some neglect or omission of duty in repairing defects or removing obstructions, must

bo established, in order to charge the municipality with
the consequences of any defects in or obstructions of
the thoroughfares within the corporation."

4. Subjects suggested. The above rule and synopsis
suggest many considerations, some of which will bo
more or less fully treated in subsequent chapters. The
arrangement of them will not perhaps be wholly logical,
but follow the sequence which seems to the writer to bo
as natural as any.

CHAPTER VI.

WHO TO BE PROTECTED, AND WHERE.

A. WHO ENTITLED TO PROTECTION.

1. New York rule. *Protection in this State is extended to every one lawfully using the streets.*

> Rehberg *v.* New York, 91 N. Y. 137.
> McGarry *v.* Loomis, 63 N. Y. 104.
> McGuire *v.* Spence, 91 N. Y. 303.
> Kunz *v.* Troy, 5 N. Y. St. R. 642.

In the case first above cited, the injury was to a workman engaged in excavating the street (so said at 91 N. Y. p. 306). In the other cases, it was to children playing.

[64]

The same rule applies in Illinois,

Chicago v. Keefe, 32 Alb. L. J. 362.

and Maryland.

Hussey v. Ryan, 4 East. R. 462.

In McGarry v. Loomis the court say :

"That it is not unlawful, wrongful or negligent for children on the sidewalk to play, is a proposition which is too plain for comment."

In Chicago v. Keefe : "Those using the streets for recreation or for pleasure, or for mere idle curiosity, so that they do not infringe upon the rights of others to use them, are equally within the protection of the law while using them, and hence equally entitled to have them in a reasonably safe condition, with those who are passing along them as travellers, or in the pursuit of their daily avocations."

2. In some States the rule prevails that only travellers are protected.

Blodgett v. Boston, 8 Allen, 237.
McCarthy v. Portland, 67 Me. 167.
Donoho v. Vulcan Iron Works, 75 Mo. 401.

But in New Hampshire, where such a rule prevails, it has been held, that for a boy to stand from three to five minutes upon a public highway to see a procession pass, does not, as matter of law, exclude him from the class of "travellers."

Varney v. Manchester, 58 N. H. 430.

5

B. THE LOCUS IN QUO.

1. Introductory. Having considered in a former chapter the somewhat abstract question of the establishment of highways, we now may notice another subject somewhat akin to that, but more intimately connected with the main subject of investigation;—for injuries received in what places must a municipal corporation respond in damages?

And first we observe that the actual establishment of a street by any of the ways heretofore considered is not always necessary to fix such liability.

2. Highway within limits. *A highway used by the public, within the limits of a municipal corporation, is a street to such an extent as to render the city liable for the consequences of an excavation made under its direction and left unguarded.*

> Brusso v. Buffalo, 90 N. Y. 679.
> Lafayette v. Larson, 73 Ind. 367.

This in New York city includes the "annexed district."

> Richard v. New York, 48 Super. 315.

And it makes no difference that the street is unflagged and unpaved.

> Bullock v. New York, 99 N. Y. 654.

3. Treated as street. *If the authorities of a city or town have treated a place as a public street, the municipality is responsible for its condition, and cannot throw the person injured into an inquiry into the manner or authority of its establishment.*

> Avery v. Syracuse, 29 Hun, 537.
> Rehberg v. New York, 91 N.Y. 137.

New York r. Sheffield, 4 Wall. 189.
Tierney v. Troy, 41 Hun, 120.

Whether a city has treated a particular place,—e. g., a causeway built by a bridge company,—as a street, is a question for the jury.

Manchester v. Ericsson, 105 U. S. 347.

4. **Right to whole street.**   Again, the question arises, must the whole street be kept safe for travel, or is the traveller restricted to any particular part?

Making due allowance for the different conditions in villages and in cities, and in more or less travelled thoroughfares; also for the necessary obstruction of portions of streets from time to time for various purposes, as before alluded to, the rule laid down in a recent New York case is a safe one.

"*As a general rule, the public are entitled not only to a free passage along the streets, but to a free passage over each and every portion of every street.*"

Lavery v. Hannigan, 52 Super. 463, at p. 467.
Monongahela v. Fischer, (Pa.) 2 Atl. R. 87.

5 **Crosswalk.**   *A crosswalk is part of the street.*

Hines v. Lockport, 50 N. Y. 236.
Walker r. Lockport, 43 How. Pr. 366.
Brusso r. Buffalo, 90 N. Y. 679.
Goodfellow r. New York, 100 N.Y. 115.
Dickinson r. New York, 92 N. Y. 584.
Detroit r. Putnam, 45 Mich. 263.

This includes a bridge over a drain at a street crossing.

Atlanta v. Champe, 66 Ga. 659.

6. **Sidewalk.** *In New York and many other States a sidewalk is part of the street.* (But see A, *supra*.)

> Graves *v.* Otis, 2 Hill, 466.
> Ellis *v.* Lowville, 7 Laus. 434.
> Fulton *v.* Tucker, 5 T. & C. 621.
> Wilson *v.* Watertown, 3 Hun, 508.
> Lavery *v.* Hannigan, 52 Super. 463.
> Koch *v.* Edgewater, 18 Hun, 407.
> Re Burmeister, 76 N. Y. 174.
> Pomfrey *v.* Saratoga Spr., 104 N. Y. 459.
> And many other New York cases.
> Providence *v.* Clapp, 17 How. (U. S.) 161.
> Cusick *v.* Norwich, 40 Conn. 375.
> Dooley *v.* Meriden, 44 Con. 117.
> Indianapolis *v.* Gaston, 58 Ind. 224.
> Tabor *v.* Graffmiller, (Ind.) 9 No. East. R. 721.

But not in others.

> Detroit *v.* Putnam, 45 Mich. 263.
> O'Neal *v.* Detroit, 50 Mich. 133.
> Dupuy *v.* Union, 46 N. J. L. 269.

The Michigan statute limits the right of action to "public highways, bridges, crosswalks and culverts."

The New Jersey act, to "insufficiency or want of repair of any public road."

Under the Michigan act, it has been held that a walk across an alley is a crosswalk and not a sidewalk.

> Pequignot *v.* Detroit, 16 Fed. Rep. 211.

Under certain charters in New York it has been held that the power of the city or village over its sidewalks is purely discretionary, and that no action will lie. See

> Cole *v.* Medina, 27 Barb. 218.
> Peck *v.* Batavia, 32 Barb. 634.
> Hart *v.* Brooklyn, 36 Barb. 226.

7. **Access from** private property. In Massachusetts, a statute exempts cities from liability for accidents in private ways leading into public ways.

This act has been held to apply to the space between the entrance to the private way and that part of the public way which is worked for travel.

Paine r. Brockton, 138 Mass. 564.

A similar statute exists in Iowa.

Goodin r. Des Moines, 55 Iowa, 67.

8. **Bridges.** In Kansas, held, that a bridge wholly within a city, is, with its approaches, a part of the street, and the same liability attaches—even though the bridge was originally built by the county.

Eudora v. Miller, 30 Kan. 494.

In New York, that if bridge and approaches, though owned by the State, are treated as part of the public street by the city, the latter is liable for their condition.

Schomer r. Rochester, 15 Abb. N. C. 57.

And the duty to keep a bridge in repair carries with it the duty to keep up guards or rails where necessary.

Hyatt v. Rondout, 44 Barb. 385.

Though this would not apply in case of a State bridge where the city had no right to place railings.

Carpenter v. Cohoes, 81 N. Y. 21.
Veeder r. Little Falls, 100 N.Y. 343.

9. Common path. For leaving unprotected a dangerous precipice, formed by cutting a road across a commonly used path, a city is liable.

Orme *v.* Richmond, 79 Va. 86.

And generally, for a commonly used path in the margin of a road, or otherwise.

Potter *r.* Castleton, 53 Vt. 435.
Aston *v.* Newton, 134 Mass. 507.

10. Apparent walk. Where a brace was put across a trench, for the purpose of supporting the soil, but apparently for a cross-walk, held that it must be kept safe.

Finegan *v.* Moore, 46 N. J. L. 602.

So must a wooden cover to a water-box in a sidewalk.

Campbell *v.* Syracuse, 20 W. Dig. 449.

11. Outside street line. Whether a cellar along the line of the street is a defect which a city is bound to remedy, ([1]) or whether a dangerous place outside the limits of the street is so near as to render the street unsafe for travel, ([2]) are questions for the jury.

([1]) Stack *v.* Portsmouth, 52 N. H. 221.
([2]) Warner *v.* Holyoke, 112 Mass. 362.
Drew *v.* Sutton, 55 Vt. 586.

Upon the question of dangers off the street, in the following cases, recovery was allowed :

(a) Person stepping one foot off the sidewalk to a hydrant two feet from the line.

Duffy r. Dubuque, 63 Iowa, 171.

(b) Excavation adjoining sidewalk, unguarded.

Bunch r. Edenton, 90 N. C. 431.

(c) Ice on pile of dirt five feet wide and a foot high, two feet off beaten track.

Stafford v. Oskaloosa, 64 Iowa, 251.

(d) Injury opposite premises occupied by plaintiff as tenant.

Avery v. Syracuse, 29 Hun, 537.

And in the following, not :

(a) Hole five feet from highway, in outskirts of village.

Keyes r. Marcellus, (Mich.) 28 Alb. L. J. 199.

(b) Place of accident, twenty-eight or thirty feet from street.

Daily r. Worcester, 131 Mass. 452.
Kelley v. Columbia, (Ohio) 31 Alb. L. J. 379.

(c) Generally, away from street.

Young v. Dist. Col., 3 MacArthur, 13/.
Barnes v. Chicopee, 138 Mass. 67.

'CHAPTER VII.

LIABILITY, HOW CONFERRED.

1. Conferred by charter. *Wherever a municipal corporation is clothed by charter with exclusive control of its streets, or its common council or trustees are empowered to care for and repair the streets; or are clothed with the powers of commissioners of highways; the corporation is liable to respond in damages to the person injured by the wrongful or negligent failure to keep such streets safe for the use of passengers thereon.*

Hutson *v.* New York, 9 N. Y. 163.
Griffin *v.* New York, 9 N. Y. 456.
Weet *v.* Brockport, 16 N. Y. 161, note.
Conrad *v.* Ithaca, 16 N. Y. 158.
Barton *v.* Syracuse, 37 Barb. 292.
Hyatt *v.* Rondout, 44 Barb. 385.

[72]

Clark v. Lockport, 49 Barb. 580.
Davenport v. Ruckman, 37 N. Y. 568.
McCarthy v. Syracuse, 46 N. Y. 194.
Requa v. Rochester, 45 N. Y. 129.
Mosey v. Troy, 61 Barb. 580.
Hines v. Lockport, 50 N. Y. 236.
Diveny v. Elmira, 51 N. Y. 506.
Todd v. Troy, 61 N. Y. 506.
Weed v. Ballston, 76 N. Y. 329.
Albrittin v. Huntsville, 60 Ala. 486.
Selma v. Perkins, 68 Ala. 145.
Chicago v. Robbins, 2 Black, 418.
Denver v. Dunsmore, 7 Col. 328.
Delger v. St. Paul, 14 Fed. Rep. 567.
Parker v. Macon, 39 Ga. 725.
Sterling v. Thomas, 60 Ill. 264.
Bohen v. Waseca, 32 Minn. 176.
Shartle v. Minneapolis, 17 Minn. 308.
Barnes v. Dist. Columbia, 91 U. S. 540.
(See also cases in different States cited in Barnes
  v. Dist. Col., at page 551 ; also in 7 U. S. Digest
  N. S., p. 594, § 150.)

The examination of this rule involves so many principles that some embarrassment arises as to the proper
order in which to consider them.

2. Liability depends on charter. *The liability of a munici-*
pal corporation to persons injured upon its streets by the
negligence of its officers depends upon the charter or statute
under which it was incorporated.

Van Vranken v. Schenectady, 31 Hun, 516.
2 Dillon Mun. Cor. § 538.
Fulton v. Tucker, 5 T. & C. 621.
Nicholls v. Minneapolis, 30 Minn. 545.

And the extent of its power and liability is wholly in
the discretion of the sovereign power.

Barnes v. Dist. Col., 91 U. S. 540.

3. Charters in New York. In New York the various cities have special charters, in some of which the common council are made commissioners of highways, in others are directly given power to repair streets, and in some both provisions are united. As stated in the rule above, the form of expression is immaterial. The villages, since 1870, are established under a general statute, which makes the village a separate highway district, and makes its trustees commissioners of highways, with power " to discontinue, lay out, open, widen, alter, change the grade or otherwise improve roads, avenues, streets, lanes, crosswalks and sidewalks."

Session Laws of 1870, p. 694, § 1.

Under this village act it has been held :

(a) That a village incorporated under it assumes the duty of caring for and repairing its streets, and for its neglect to do so is liable to a party injured.

Nelson v. Canisteo, 100 N. Y. 89.

(b) But is not under obligation to repair bridges,— that that remains in the town.

Washburn v. Mount Kisco, 35 Hun, 329.

4. Municipalities exempt by charter. From the fact that the liability is statutory, it follows that it may be limited by statute. This is in fact the case in various municipalities in this State, — for instance, in Brooklyn, Binghamton, Schenectady and Ogdensburgh.

(a) In Brooklyn it is provided that "The city of Brooklyn shall not be liable in damages for any misfeasance or non-feasance of the common council, or any officer of the city or appointee of the common council, of any duty imposed upon them or any or either of them, by the provisions of this act, or of any other duty enjoined upon them or any or either of them, as officers of government, by any provision of this act; but the remedy . . shall be . . . against the members of the common council, officer or appointee . . . if at all.".

Session Laws of 1873, p. 1378, § 27.

The constitutionality of this act was attacked in Gray v. Brooklyn, 50 Barb. 365; 2 Abb. Dec. 267, upon the ground that it impaired the obligation of a contract. It was declared constitutional upon the ground that 'the acceptance of its original charter (Laws 1854, p. 860, § 1), in which the power over highways was vested in the common council, was not a contract with the person injured, but between the city and the State, by whose sovereign act the charter had been conferred.

In that case, the court went so far as to hold that "The object of the legislature is clear, and that was to exonerate the city from liability on account of the omission and misconduct of its officers, and to impose all the legal consequences of their acts directly upon the persons who might be guilty of such official misconduct."

The full force put upon this statute in Gray v. Brooklyn has been somewhat modified in later cases. Such are:

Fitzpatrick v. Slocum, 89 N. Y. 358.
Hardy v. Brooklyn, 90 N. Y. 435.
Vincent v. Brooklyn, 31 Hun, 122.

In Fitzpatrick *v.* Slocum the court say :

"There must be a remedy where one is injured without fault of his own by a defect in one of the streets or bridges of the city, either against the city or some one of its officers. The primary duty to keep its streets and bridges in safe condition rests upon the city, and there is a general obligation upon it to use proper care and vigilance in putting and keeping its streets and bridges in safe condition, and unless that duty has been plainly devolved upon some officer or officers of the city against whom a remedy for non-feasance can be had, the remedy is against the city upon its obligation. *That section does not exempt the city from liability to discharge a duty resting upon it, and which it has not devolved upon any one of its officers.*"

(b) The Binghamton charter differs from that of Brooklyn, in this respect only, in that in Binghamton there is no liability of the officer, except in case of gross negligence.

Session Laws of 1867, p. 651, § 6.

Under this it was held, in Fitzgerald *v.* Binghamton, 40 Hun, 332, that the reasoning of Fitzpatrick *v.* Slocum applied there with still greater force, since gross negligence of the officer did not appear, and hence there could be no remedy but against the city ; and the three later Brooklyn cases were followed.

(c) The Ogdensburgh charter makes the common council commissioners of highways, but relieves the city from liability to a person injured " by any defect in the plan upon or in the manner in which any sidewalk in said city shall be constructed, or by reason of the same not being in repair, or by slipping upon any snow or ice thereon."

Session Laws of 1881, ch. 95, p. 112.

Under this it was held in Piercy v. Averill, 37 Hun, 360, that the members of the common council may be liable to the person injured.

(d) The Schenectady charter declares that the city shall not be liable for injuries sustained by defective sidewalks, unless actual notice of the defect shall have been given to the common council or superintendent of streets at least twenty-four hours previous to the injury. It also provides that claims must be presented within three months; and actions brought within a year.

Laws of 1882, p. 359, ch. 294, § 4.

This act was declared constitutional in

Van Vranken v. Schenectady, 31 Hun, 516.

following Gray v. Brooklyn, *supra.*

5. **Liability based on agreement.** *The theory upon which the liability of a municipality to the person injured is said to be based is that of an agreement or contract, express or implied, between the sovereign power and the corporation, by which the former confers valuable franchises and powers, and the latter becomes bound to certain corresponding duties.*

Cain v. Syracuse, 29 Hun, 105.
Ensign v. Livingston Co., 25 Hun, 20.
Weet v. Brockport, 16 N. Y. 161, note.
Maxmilian v. New York, 62 N.Y. 160.

Buffalo *v.* Yattan, 1 Buff. Super. Ct. 485.
Aldrich *v.* Tripp, 11 R. I. 14.
Omaha *v.* Olmstead, 5 Neb. 446.

In Ensign *v.* Livingston Co. Supervisors the court say :

"The surrender by the government of a portion of its sovereign power to the municipality, if accepted by the latter, has been regarded as affording a consideration for an implied agreement, on the part of the corporation, to perform the duties imposed by the charter, a neglect of which will render the corporation liable . . . to a private action at the suit of a person injured by such neglect."

In Weet *v.* Brockport :

"Whenever an individual or a corporation, for a consideration received from the sovereign power, has become bound by covenant or agreement, express or implied, to do certain things, such individual or corporation is liable, in case of neglect to perform such covenant, to the person injured."

In Maxmilian *v.* New York :

"The duty of keeping in repair streets, bridges and other common ways of passage, and a liability for a neglect to perform that duty, rest upon an express or implied acceptance of the power and an agreement to do so. It is a duty with which the city is charged for its own corporate benefit, to be performed by its own agents, as its own corporate act."

6. Power implies duty. In New York the principle has been long recognized that :

> " *Where a public body or officer is clothed with power to do an act which concerns the public interest or the rights of third persons, the execution of the power may be insisted on as a duty, though the statute creating it be only permissive in its terms.*"

This is illustrated in the following, among many cases.

New York *v.* Furze, 3 Hill, 612.
Hines *v.* Lockport, 60 Barb. 378.
Hutson *v.* New York, 9 N. Y. 163.
Rehberg *v.* New York, 91 N. Y. 137.
Nebraska City *v.* Campbell, 2 Black, 590.

7. Theory of agency. *The liability of a municipal corporation for the negligent performance of a duty imposed upon its trustees or common council, is based upon the doctrine that such officers are, in their capacity as commissioners of highways, to be regarded as agents of the corporation.*

Conrad *v.* Ithaca, 16 N. Y. 158.
Hyatt *v.* Rondout, 44 Barb. 385.
Todd *v.* Troy, 61 N. Y. 506.
Weed *v.* Ballston, 76 N. Y. 329.
Sowell *v.* Cohoes, 75 N. Y. 45.

And other cases cited under (1) *supra*.

8. Liability dependent on funds. *The absence of the necessary funds, and of the legal means of procuring them, will excuse* *the non-performance of the duty of a municipal corporation to keep its streets safe for travel.*

> Hines *v.* Lockport, 50 N. Y. 236.
> Peach *v.* Utica, 10 Hun, 477.
> Albrittin *v.* Huntsville, 60 Ala. 486.
> Delger *v.* St. Paul, 14 Fed. Rep. 567.
> Shartle *v.* Minneapolis, 17 Minn. 308.

But absence of funds alone will not excuse, provided the city has power to raise funds.

> Peach *v.* Utica, *supra.*
> La Duke *v.* Fultonville, 20 W. Dig. 453.
> Pomfrey *v.* Saratoga, 34 Hun, 607.
> Ellis *v.* Lowville, 7 Lans. 434.

The same rule and exception applied with respect to the liability of highway commissioners under the old law in New York, (¹) and that of towns under the act of 1881.(²)

> (¹) Adsit *v.* Brady, 4 Hill, 630.
> Hover *v.* Barkhoof, 44 N. Y. 113.
> Warren *v.* Clement, 24 Hun, 472.
> Smith *v.* Wright, 24 Barb. 170.
> Garlinghouse *v.* Jacobs, 29 N. Y. 297.
> (²) Eveleigh *v.* Hounsfield, 34 Hun, 140.
> Monk *v.* New Utrecht, 104 N. Y. 552.

(a) *Burden of proof.* In Eveleigh v. Hounsfield, *supra*, it was held that the burden of alleging and proving funds in a town is upon the person seeking to recover against the town.

The three cases cited as sustaining that doctrine are People v. Adsit, 2 Hill, 619, and Garlinghouse v. Jacobs, and Warren v. Clement, *supra.*

Upon examination it would seem that this position is sustained by only the first of those cases, in which the question arose upon the sufficiency of an *indictment*, and it was thus distinguished in Adsit *v.* Brady, *infra.*

In the following cases it was held that the burden of proving lack of funds was upon the defendant.

> Adsit *v.* Brady, 4 Hill, 630.
> Ellis *v.* Lowville, 7 Lans. 434.
> Weed *v.* Ballston, 76 N. Y. at p. 335.
> Hines *v.* Lockport, 50 N. Y. 236.
> Day *v.* Crossman, 1 Hun, 570.
> Hover *v.* Barkhoof, 44 N. Y. 113, at p. 118.
> Pomfrey *v.* Saratoga, 34 Hun, 607.

For the purpose of showing funds, it is proper to prove the making of repairs the day after the accident.

> Morrell *v.* Peck, 88 N. Y. 398.

6

CHAPTER VIII.

PUBLIC AND CORPORATE FUNCTIONS.

1. Dual powers.
2. Care of streets a corporate duty.
3. Discretionary acts.
4. Negligent plan.
5. Ministerial acts.
6. Care of excavations, &c!
7. *Quasi* corporations.

1. Dual powers. *A municipal corporation possesses two kinds of functions; one governmental and political in their character, and solely for the public benefit and protection, the other private, exercising as a corporation, private franchise powers and privileges, which belong to it for its immediate corporate benefit. While in the exercise of the former the corporation is a municipal government, and while in the exercise of the latter is a corporate, legal individual.*

Lloyd *v.* New York, 5 N. Y. 369.
Wilson *v.* New York, 1 Denio, 595.
Bailey *v.* New York, 3 Hill, 531.
Rochester White Lead Company *v.* Rochester, 3
    N. Y. 463.
Maxmilian *v.* New York, 62 N. Y. 160.
Welsh *v.* Rutland, 67 Vt. 228.
Hill *v.* Boston, 122 Mass. 344.
Eastman *v.* Meredith, 36 N. H. 284.
Mills *v.* Brooklyn, 32 N. Y. 489.

Radcliff's Ex'rs *v.* New York, 4 N. Y. 195.
Hines *v.* Lockport, 50 N. Y. 236.
Little Rock *v.* Willis, 27 Ark, 572.
Elgin *v.* Kimball, 90 Ill. 356.
(See also many cases cited in briefs in Clemence *v.*
    Auburn, 66 N. Y. 334.)

In the exercise of the former kind it is said that a
corporation acts in a judicial or semi-judicial capacity,
under the latter in an administrative ; that it is not
responsible to a person injured by its manner of exercising the former, but of the latter it is.

The principle in both its branches is excellently
stated, with citations of authorities, in the opinion in
Hines *v.* Lockport, 50 N. Y. at p. 238 :

"Where power is conferred on public officers, or a
municipal corporation, to make improvements,—such as
streets, sewers, &c., and keep them in repair,—the duty
to make them is *quasi*-judicial or discretionary, involving
a determination as to their necessity, requisite capacity,
location, &c., and for a failure to exercise this power, or
an erroneous estimate of the public needs, no civil action
is maintainable. But when this discretion has been exercised, and the street, sewer, or other improvement has
been made, the duty to keep it in repair, so as to prevent it from being dangerous to the public, is ministerial, and for a negligent omission to perform this duty, an
action lies by the party injured."

2. Care of streets a corporate duty. *The duty which the
city owes to the traveller to keep its streets in a safe condition*

84   LAW.

for public travel, is a corporate as distinguished from a governmental duty.

> Ehrgott v. New York, 96 N. Y. 264.
> Conrad v. Ithaca, 16 N. Y. 158.
> Maxmilian v. New York, 62 N. Y. 160.

3. Discretionary acts. *It may be said, generally, that a municipal corporation is not liable for the plans adopted by it in the making of public improvements, (^{1}) or for the exercise of its discretion as to what improvements shall be made, or for its municipal regulations generally.(^{2})*

> (^{1}) Toolan v. Lansing, 38 Mich, 315.
> Bannagan v. Dist. Col., 2 Mackey, 285.
> Rozell v. Anderson, 91 Ind. 591.
> (^{2}) Henderson v. Sandefur, 11 Bush (Ky.) 550.
> Cole v. Medina, 27 Barb. 218.

Thus it can incur no liability for failure to open, fill, or grade streets,

> Lynch v. New York, 76 N. Y. 60.
> Hughes v. Baltimore, Taney, 243.

or to construct sidewalks,

> Saulsbury v. Ithaca, 24 Hun, 12; 94 N. Y. 27.

or cross-walks,

> Williams v. Grand Rapids, (Mich.) 33 Alb. L. J. 237.
> Easton v. Neff, (Pa.) 29 Alb. L. J. 372.

or improve streets in sparsely-settled parts,

> Henderson v. Sandefur, 11 Bush (Ky.) 550.

or light streets,

> Lyon *r.* Cambridge, 136 Mass. 419.
> Freeport *c.* Isbell, 83 Ill. 440.

or appoint inspectors of steam boilers,

> Mead *v.* New Haven. 40 Conn. 72.

or superintendents of streets,

> King *v.* Chapin, 23 W. Dig. 528.

or make ordinances,

> Rochester White Lead Co. *v* Rochester, 3 N. Y. 463.

or construct sewers.

> Kavanagh *v.* Brooklyn, 38 Barb. 232.
> Mills *v.* Brooklyn, 32 N. Y. 489.
> Wilson *v.* New York, 1 Denio, 595.

It is not liable for altering the grade of a sidewalk,

> Kavanagh *v.* Brooklyn, *supra.*
> Waddell *r.* New York, 8 Barb. 95.

or for the plan of a sidewalk,

> Urquhart *r.* Ogdensburgh, 91 N. Y. 67 ; 97 Id. 238.
> Watson *v.* Kingston, 26 W. Dig. 15.

or of a sewer,

> Hardy *r.* Brooklyn, 7 Abb. N. C. 403.

or for regulating the cleaning of sewers,

> Lloyd *v.* New York, 5 N. Y. 369.

or for blasting rocks for sewers, in absence of negligence.

Murphy v. Lowell, 128 Mass. 396.

In Urquhart v. Ogdensburgh, 91 N. Y. 67, it was held that the approval of the plan of a sidewalk made by an individual was as much a judicial act as the design of it.

In the same case, on a second appeal (97 N. Y. 238), it was held that approval cannot be assumed from failure to disapprove.

See also Garrett v. Buffalo, 26 Week. Dig. 257.

4. **Negligent plan.** A municipal corporation is liable for *negligence* in the plan of an improvement, as well as in the manner of executing the work.

North Vernon v. Voegler, (Ind.) 2 No. E. R. 82 ; 32 Alb. L. J. 466.
Ferguson v. Davis County, 57 Iowa, 601.
Gould v. Topeka, 32 Kan. 485.
Rice v. Evansville, (Ind.) 35 Alb. L. J. 138.

A similar principle seems to have been recognized in Clemence v. Auburn, 66 N. Y. 334, where a portion of a sidewalk had been built on a new grade, and, at the place where the new part approached the old, a stone had been placed with a much steeper grade than the rest of the walk. This had been directed by the chairman of the street committee of the common council, and the court held it not a judicial act, upon the ground that there could be no presumption of authority in the officer.

But the court say :

"It is questionable whether, the absolute duty being imposed by law upon the city to construct and keep in repair the sidewalks, the city would not be liable to any one travelling thereon for injuries resulting from an improper construction of the walks, whether in respect to grade, material or other thing; in other words, whether, the duty being conceded, it is not absolute to make them reasonably safe for public travel."

In Hubbell v. Yonkers, 35 Hun, 349, the injury was caused by a frightened horse going over an unprotected embankment beside the street, some twelve feet high, and which had been there ten years.

The court, after citing some cases to the effect that a city is not liable for the plan of construction of its streets, say :

"These cases do not decide that a municipal corporation may escape liability for a defective construction of an improvement, merely because it is made in accordance with an approved plan. If a bridge over a ravine or a water stream was built by a city or a village, and left without a side guard, or a street was constructed on a causeway high above the natural level of the ground, and left without side rails or protection, responsibility for injuries resulting from their absence could not be avoided by showing that they were made in accordance with the plans.

" Such a doctrine, carried to its legitimate conclusion and result, might release all municipal corporations from the duty imposed on them to maintain the streets within their limits in a safe condition for travel in the usual modes."

In North Vernon v. Voegler, the court say :

" Suppose that a common council of a city determine
to build a sewer and cover it with reeds, can it be possible that the corporation can escape liability on the
ground that the common council erred in devising a
plan ?

" Or suppose the common council undertake to conduct a large volume of water through a culvert capable
of carrying less than one-tenth of the water conducted
to it by the drains constructed by the city, can responsibility be evaded on the ground of an error of
judgment ?

" Again, ... suppose the common council to
devise a plan for· a bridge, that will require tim-
bers so slight as to give way beneath the tread of a
child, can the city escape liability on the ground
that there was only an error of judgment in devising
the plan?"

5. **Ministerial acts.** *When the discretionary power of a
municipal corporation is put in exercise, it is responsible for
the manner of performance.*

Barton *v.* Syracuse, 37 Barb. 292.
Ludlow *v.* Yonkers, 43 Barb. 493.
Lacour *v.* N. Y., 3 Duer, 406.
Rochester White Lead Co. *v.* Rochester, 3 N. Y.
    463.
Buffalo and Hamburgh Turnpike Co. *v.* Buffalo,
    1 T. & C. 537.
Piercy *v.* Averill, 37 Hun, 360.
Nims *v.* Troy, 59 N. Y. 500.

McCarthy r. Syracuse, 46 N. Y. 194.
Hubbell r. Yonkers, 35 Hun, 349.
McDonough r. Virginia City, 6 Nev. 90.
Hines r. Lockport, 50 N. Y. 236.

6. Care of excavations, etc. Important illustrations of the above rule occur in case of excavations, &c., made or permitted in the streets. As has been commented on before, it is necessary that the obstructing of the street for building purposes and the excavating it for various purposes, partly by the city itself, partly by its licensees, should be done. The fact of obstructing in the one case, in the other of permitting, is not in itself necessarily wrongful; but under such circumstances the city is " bound to protect all prudent persons against accident."

Covington v. Bryant, 7 Bush (Ky.) 248.
See also Lacour v. New York, 3 Duer, 406.
Storrs v. Utica, 17 N. Y. 104.
Brusso r. Buffalo, 90 N. Y. 679.
Grant r. Brooklyn, 41 Barb. 381.
Platz r. Cohoes, 89 N. Y. 219.
Osborn v. Union Ferry Co., 53 Barb. 629.
Port Jervis r. First Nat. Bk., 96 N. Y. 550.
Groves v. Rochester, 39 Hun, 5.
McMahon v. Second Ave. R. R. Co., 75 N. Y. 231.
Seneca Falls r. Zalinski, 8 Hun, 571.
Lemont v. Rood, 18 Bradw. (Ill. Ap.) 245.

7. Quasi-corporations. *The distinction is taken that it is the governmental power alone that is possessed by counties and towns, which, like assembly and senatorial districts, school districts, &c., are merely political divisions organized for the convenient exercise of the political power of the State.*

Ensign r. Livingston Co., 25 Hun, 20.
People ex rel. Loomis r. Little Valley, 75 N. Y. 316.
Morey r. Newfane, 8 Barb. 645.

And in California the same is true of cities.

> Winbigler v. Los Angeles, 45 Cal. 36.
> Tranter v. Sacramento, 61 Cal. 271.

These are often called *quasi* corporations.

> Barnes v. District of Columbia, 91 U. S. 540.
> Donalson v. San Miguel Co., 1 New Mex. 263.

While a liability is under many jurisdictions imposed upon these *quasi* corporations with regard to repair of streets, it is always expressly prescribed by statute, under the sovereign power of the State. The element of liability to be implied from a power, under an agreement, upon a consideration, is wanting.

Illustrative of the liability thus imposed by statute upon political divisions may be mentioned several of the New England and other States, in which the care of roads and bridges is vested in the several towns, and a cause of action is expressly given by statute against a town for neglect of repair. But the courts in those States hold that no action lies except by force of the statute giving it.

> Bigelow v. Randolph, 14 Gray, 541.
> Chidsey v. Canton, 17 Conn. 475.
> Reed v. Belfast, 20 Maine, 246.
> Eastman v. Meredith, 36 N. H. 284.
> Frazer v. Lewiston, 76 Me. 531.
> Altnow v. Sibley, 30 Minn. 186.
> Yeager v. Tippecanoe, 81 Ind. 46.

It follows that in absence of such a statute there is no liability to the person injured.

> Ensign v. Livingston Co., 25 Hun, 20.
> White v. Chowan Co. Comrs., 90 N. C. 437.
> Clark v. Adair Co., 79 Mo. 536.

In New York, prior to 18.1, the only remedy of persons injured upon town highways was against the commissioners of highways.

By Session Laws of 1881, ch. 700, this liability in the first instance was transferred to the town, with right of recovery over against the commissioners in case the injury is caused by their negligence.

This act was held constitutional in

Bidwell *v.* Murray, 40 Hun, 190.

But that it is not retroactive in its effect, in

Frasier *r.* Tompkins, 30 Hun, 168.

CHAPTER IX.

FOR WHOSE ACTS LIABLE.

A. AGENTS AND SERVANTS.

1. In general. That a municipal corporation is liable to the individual injured by the act or neglect of its servants or agents is but saying that it is responsible for its own act or neglect, since it can act only through them.

[92]

The acts of agents which bind the corporation are not, however, without limitation; and questions often arise as to the persons for whose acts the city is liable under the doctrine of *respondeat superior*.

2. Ultra vires. *A municipal corporation is not liable to an individual whose injury is the result of illegal acts of its agents or officers.*

> Boom *v.* Utica, 2 Barb. 104.
> Albany *v.* Cunliff, 2 N. Y. 165.
> Herrington *v.* Corning, 51 Barb. 396.
> Smith *v.* Rochester, 76 N. Y. 506.
> Davies *v.* New York, 4 Civ. Pro. 290.

In Boom *v.* Utica, the common council, assuming a power to do so from the charter provisions for the removal of nuisances, ordered the placing of certain persons, sick with a contagious disease, in a building owned by the plaintiff, without his consent. Held, *ultra vires*, and that no recovery could be had against the city.

In Albany *v.* Cunliff, the officer and agents of a city assumed to build a bridge by authority of an unconstitutional statute. The bridge fell by reason of its negligent construction. Held, that a person injured had no remedy against the city.

In Herrington *v.* Corning, the injury was caused by the decayed condition of a sidewalk, which the village trus-

tees had constructed contrary to the provision of the
statute of incorporation.

B.   INDEPENDENT OFFICERS AND DEPARTMENTS.

1. When city not liable. *A municipal corporation is not
liable for the wrongful or negligent acts of public officers or
departments (or their employees), whose duties are prescribed
by the State, who are not under the supervision of the corporation, and whose duties do not enure to the corporate benefit;
though they be appointed by the corporation.   Thus held of*

Fire department.

> Burrill *v.* Augusta, (Me.) 4 Eastern Reporter,
>   615.
> Wild *v.* Paterson, (N. J.) 2 Eastern Reporter,
>   808.
> Woolbridge *v.* New York, 49 How. Pr. 67.
> Robinson *v.* Evansville, 87 Ind. 334.
> McKenna *v.* St. Louis, 6 Mo. Ap. 320.

Member or employee of fire department.

> Smith *v.* Rochester, 76 N. Y. 506.
> Wilcox *v.* Chicago, 107 Ill. 334 ; 29 Alb. L. J.
>   37.
> Freeman *v.* Philadelphia, 13 Phila. 154.
> Welsh *v.* Rutland, 56 Vt. 228 ; 30 Alb. L. J.
>   163.
> Edgerly *v.* Concord, 59 N. H. 78, 341.

Police department.

> Sinclair *v.* Baltimore, 59 Md. 592.

Policeman.

McKay *v.* Buffalo, 9 Hun. 401 ; 74 N. Y. 619.
Citing Stewart *v.* New Orleans, 9 La. An.
461.
Buttrick *v.* Lowell, 1 Allen, 172.
Dargan *v.* Mobile, 31 Ala. 469.
Kunz *v.* Troy, 36 Hun, 615, distinguishing Reh-
berg *v.* New York, 91 N. Y. 137.

Department of public instruction.

Ham *v.* New York, 70 N. Y. 459.

Board of health.

Bamber *v.* Rochester, 26 Hun, 587.

Board of revision and correction of assessments.

Tone *v.* New York, 70 N. Y. 157.

Department of buildings.

Connors *v.* New York, 11 Hun, 439.

Department of docks.

Bigler *v.* New York, 5 Abb. N. C. 51.

Commissioners of charities and correction.

Maxmilian *v.* New York, 62 N. Y. 160.
(Principal case.)

Servant of board of public works.

Condict *v.* Jersey City, 46 N. J. L. 157.

96   LAW.

Commissioners to build docks in canal.

> New York *v.* Lumber Co., 71 N. Y. 580.

Mayor of city.

> Cumberland *v.* Willison, 50 Md. 138.

Trustees of village.

> Martin *v.* New York, 1 Hill, 545.

Fire insurance patrol.

> Boyd *v.* Insurance Patrol of Philadelphia, 35 Alb.
> L. J. 218.

2. When city liable. (a) *But is liable when it has the appointment and supervision, and when the duty to be performed is for the benefit of the corporation.*

Engineers and water commissioners.

> New York *v.* Bailey, 2 Denio, 433.

Board of health.

> Tormey *v.* New York, 12 Hun, 542.

Trustees of Brooklyn bridge.

> Walsh *v.* New York, 41 Hun, 299.

(b) *And where the duty is imposed on the corporation, and the officers or departments are simply made by charter agents of the corporation.*

> Martin *v.* New York, *supra.*
> Polley *v.* Buffalo, 20 W. Dig. 163.

Commissioners of public works.

> Niven v. Rochester, 76 N. Y. 619.

Board of public works.

> Barnes v. District of Columbia, 91 U. S. 540.

Park Commissioners.

> Ehrgott v. New York, 96 N. Y. 264.

Commissioners of water-works.

> Deyoo v. Saratoga, 3 T. & C. 504.

Executive board.

> Groves v. Rochester, 39 Hun. 5.

Water board.

> Pettengill v. Yonkers, 25 W. Dig. 45.

3. Respondeat superior. This non-liability for acts of independent officers and departments is based on the doctrine of *respondeat superior*, which presupposes a power to control and direct the persons at fault. Liability, where it exists, "is based upon the right which the employer has to select his servants, to discharge them if not competent, or skillful, or well-behaved, and to direct and control them while in his employ (Kelly v. New York, 11 N. Y. 432). The rule has no application to a case in which this power does not exist (Blake v. Ferris, 5 N. Y. 48)."

> Maxmilian v. New York, 62 N. Y. 160. at p. 163.

7

C. INDEPENDENT CONTRACTORS.

1. **Work not dangerous.** It is a well established general rule, that where work not of itself dangerous is being done under contract, if there is any negligence, it is that of the contractors or persons under them, and they are alone responsible.

" *Where the obstruction or defect caused or created in the street is purely collateral to the work contracted to be done, and is entirely the result of the wrongful acts of the the contractor or his workmen, the rule is that the employer is not liable.*"

> Water Company *v.* Ware, 16 Wall. 566, at p. 576.
> Dressell *v.* Kingston, 32 Hun, 526, at p. 535.
> Blake *v.* Ferris, 5 N. Y. 48.
> Pack *v.* New York, 8 N. Y. 222,
> Kelly *v.* New York, 11 N. Y. 432.
> Buffalo *v.* Holloway, Seld. Notes, 25.
> King *v.* N. Y. C. & H. R. R. Co., 66 N. Y. 181.
> McCafferty *v.* Spuyten Duyvil, &c. R. R. Co., 61 N. Y. 178.
> Pierrepont *v.* Loveless, 72 N. Y. 211.
> Martin *v* Tribune Asn., 30 Hun, 391.
> Gourdier *v.* Cormack, 2 E. D. Smith, 254.
> Gardner *v.* Bennett, 38 Super. 197.
> Burmeister *v.* N. Y. El. R. R. Co. 47 Super. 264.
> East St. Louis *v.* Giblin, 3 Ill. Ap. 219.
> Herrington *v.* Lansingburgh, 36 Hun, 598.

In Blake *v.* Ferris, the defendants were licensees to construct a sewer in a street, who contracted with another person to do the work, and the injury happened through the negligence of the latter in leaving the excavation open and unguarded. It was held as above ; also, that a stipulation for guarding contained in the license did not enure to the benefit of the person injured, as against the licensee.

In Pack v. New York, the city was held not liable for the negligence of a sub-contractor in conducting the blasting of rock so that pieces of rock struck a house and injured its inmates.

Also held, that a clause providing that the contractor should conform to further directions of the corporation, referred only to *results*, not to *methods*, and did not change the relation so as to make the contractor and his workmen agents of the city.

2. Supervision by officers. The above rule is in accordance with the doctrine of *respondeat superior*. Upon the same principle it is further held that :

The rule is not otherwise, although the contract provides that the work should be done under the direction and to the satisfaction of certain officers of the corporation, or other person selected for that purpose.

> Kelly v. New York, 11 N. Y. 432.
> Gardner v. Bennett, 38 Super. 197.
> Groves v. Rochester, 39 Hun, 5.
> Clare v. Nat'l City Bank, 40 Super. 104.
> Herrington v. Lansingburgh, 36 Hun, 598.
> School District of Erie v. Fuess, (Pa.) 25 Alb. L.
> J. 136.

3. Work dangerous. *Where, however, the injury is not caused by the negligent way in which the work is done, but is the result of the work itself, contracted for, however skillfully performed, then the principal is liable.*

"When the obstruction or defect which occasioned the injury results directly from the acts which the con-

tractor agreed and was authorized to do, the person who
employs the contractor and authorizes him to do those
acts, is equally liable to the injured party."

> Water Company *v.* Ware, 16 Wall. 566.
> Dressel *v.* Kingston, 32 Hun, 526.
> Storrs *v.* Utica, 17 N. Y. 104.
> McCafferty *v.* Spuyten Duyvil R. R. Co., 61 N. Y.
>   178.
> Baxter *v.* Warner, 6 Hun, 585.
> Lockwood *v.* New York, 2 Hilton, 66.
> Maxmilian *v.* New York, 62 N. Y. 160.
> Lacour *v.* New York, 3 Duer, 406.
> Hawxhurst *v.* New York, 43 Hun, 588.
> Robbins *v.* Chicago, 4 Wall. 657.
> Joliet *v.* Harwood, 86 Ill. 110.
> Circleville *v.* Neuding, 41 Ohio St. 465.
> Prentiss *v.* Boston, 112 Mass. 43.
> Baltimore *v.* O'Donnell, 53 Md. 110.
> Logansport *v.* Dick, 70 Ind. 65.

In Storrs *v.* Utica, and Dressel *v.* Kingston, the
injury was caused by an unprotected excavation left by
employees of a contractor. The court say, in the former
case, and quote in the latter: "The performance of the
work necessarily renders the street unsafe for night
travel. This is a result which does not at all depend on
the care or negligence of the laborers employed by the
contractor. The danger arises from the very nature of
the improvement; and if it can be averted only by special
precaution, such as placing guards or lighting the street,
the corporation which has authorized the work is plainly
bound to take these precautions."

4. **Primary duty of city to care for streets.** In applying
the principle of the non-liability of a municipal corporation for the acts of an independent contractor, there must

always be borne in mind the primary duty resting upon such corporations to care for their streets.

The position of a municipal corporation in respect to work upon its streets is well stated in a Tennessee case :

"*It is the duty of the corporation to use care and vigilance in the selection of agents, servants and contractors, in making improvements, to retain the requisite degree of control and superintendence over them in the performance of their duty ; and to enforce such measures of vigilance and care as will guard against exposure to injuries of any kind.*"

Nashville *v.* Brown, 9 Heisk. 1.

And in Rhode Island :

"The duty resting upon a town or city to keep its highways safe and convenient for travel is a public duty, and it has no power, unless authorized by statute, to divest itself, either by contract or ordinance, of its capacity to discharge this duty."

Watson *v.* Tripp, 11 R. I. 98.

In accordance with these principles it has been held in New York and other States that :

"A municipal corporation, owing to the public the duty of keeping its streets in a safe condition for travel, is liable to persons receiving injury from the neglect to keep proper lights and guards at night around an excavation which it has caused to be made in the street, whether it has or has not contracted for such precautions with the persons executing the work."

Storrs *v.* Utica, 17 N. Y. 104.
Osborn *v.* Union Ferry Co., 53 Barb. 629.
Dressel *v.* Kingston, 32 Hun, 526.
Buffalo *v.* Holloway, 7 N. Y. 493.
Welsh *v.* St. Louis, 73 Mo. 71 ; 25 Alb. L. J. 137.
Jacksonville *v.* Drew, 19 Flor. 106.
Wilson *v.* Wheeling, 19 W. Va. 323.

In the last case cited, held, that a city is liable in such a case, though it had no control over the workmen, and had made a contract by which the contractor assumed all liability for accidents.

D. LICENSEES.

1. License lawful. *Consent by a municipal corporation, in pursuance of lawful authority, to a citizen to excavate or obstruct a public street, does not make it responsible for the wrongful or negligent manner in which its licensee and his employees do the work.*

Port Jervis *v.* First Nat'l Bank, 96 N. Y. 550.
Masterton *v.* Mount Vernon, 58 N. Y. 391.
Dorlon *v.* Brooklyn, 46 Barb, 604.
James' Adm'x *v.* Harrodsburgh, (Ky.) 35 A. L. J. 386.
Scanlon *v.* New York, 12 Daly, 81.

2. Injury by mode of exercise. *So even if the granting of the license were unlawful, but the injury result from the negligent mode in which the licensee exercised the privilege granted to him, such mode of exercise being no part of the thing licensed.*

Cohen *v.* New York, 33 Hun, 404.
See 43 Hun, 345.

In that case the license was to keep a wagon on the street in front of a grocery store. The licensee kept the wagon near the curb with the thills turned up and fastened with a string. A passing wagon struck the wagon and broke the string, whereby the thills fell and killed a person walking on the sidewalk.

3. License for dangerous thing. *Where, however, the license was unlawful and the injury was a result of it, the licensor would undoubtedly be liable.*

> Estelle *v.* Lake Crystal, 27 Minn. 243.
> Little *v.* Madison, 42 Wis. 643.

In the former case, the injury was caused by a platform which had been built in a street with consent of the city; in the latter, the city licensed an exhibition of bears in the street, at which horses were frightened.

4. Subject to duty as to streets. *The rule first above stated is subject to the general liability of the corporation to keep its streets safe for travel. And the fact of the permit is more or less evidence of notice to the city.*

Upon this general ground, cities have often been held liable for injuries caused by obstructions or excavations created by their licensees.

> Davenport *v.* Ruckman, 37 N. Y. 568.
> Wendell *v.* Troy, 4 Keyes, 261.
> Masterton *v.* Mt. Vernon, 58 N. Y. 391.
> Indianapolis *v.* Doherty, 71 Ind. 5.
> Russell *v.* Columbia, 74 Mo. 480.
> Cusick *v.* Norwich, 40 Conn. 375.
> Savannah *v.* Donnelly, 71 Ga. 258.
> Campbell *v.* Stillwater, (Minn.) 31 Alb. L. J. 119.
> Wilson *v.* Watertown, 5 T. & C. 579 ; 3 Hun, 508.
> People *ex rel.* Markey *v.* Brooklyn, 65 N. Y. 349.
> Hirsch *v.* Buffalo, 21 W. Dig. 312.

In each of the four last cases cited, the injury was caused by the act of a railroad company, which, as a condition of laying tracks in the street, assumed the duty of keeping them safe. Held, that this did not relieve the city of its obligation for care in keeping the streets safe for travel.

In Indianapolis v. Doherty, the court say:

"When the city issues a building permit to use and obstruct a street, it is the duty of the corporate authorities to see to it that the person she authorizes to use her streets shall properly guard and protect such obstruction."

And in Masterton v. Mt. Vernon:

"Where the officers of a municipal corporation, in pursuance of a lawful authority, give permission to a lot-owner to connect his lot with a sewer, such officers are required to exercise reasonable care to prevent injury, and for the omission thereof the corporation is liable."

E.   OTHER PERSONS.

1. Depends on notice. *Speaking generally, a city is not liable for the acts of persons acting without license, except after due notice to charge it under its general liability to keep streets in safe condition for travel.*

Griffin v. New York, 9 N. Y. 456.
McGinity v. New York, 5 Duer, 674.
Hunt v. New York, 52 Super. 198.
Lafayette v. Blood, 40 Ind. 62.
Fort Wayne v. Dewitt, 47 Ind. 391.
Joliet v. Seward, 86 Ill. 402.
Otto v. Wolf, 106 Pa. St. 608.
Warren v. Wright, 3 Ill. Ap. 602.

But with notice, liable.

Aurora *v.* Bitner, 100 Ind. 396.
Barnes *v.* Newton, 46 Iowa, 567.
Moore *v.* Minneapolis, 19 Minn. 300.

2. Acceptance by city. If the structure made by another be adopted by the city, then the city becomes liable exactly as though it had been built by itself.

Johnson *v.* Milwaukee, 46 Wis. 568.
Hill *v.* Fond du Lac, 56 Wis. 242.
Hiller *v.* Sharon Springs, 28 Hun, 341.
Oliver *v.* Kansas City, 69 Mo. 79.

CHAPTER X.

PROXIMATE CAUSE.

1. Introductory.
2. Two proximate causes.
3. Application to city-negligence cases.
4. Runaway horses.

1. Introductory. It need hardly be mentioned that the negligence or wrongful act, for injuries arising from which an individual may recover, must have been a proximate cause of that injury. In practice, however, some difficulty may present itself in the application of this rule.

2. Two proximate causes. *Where two or more proximate causes contribute to an accident, and each is an efficient cause without the operation of which the accident would not have happened, it may be attributed to all or any of the causes ; but it cannot be attributed to a cause unless without its operation the accident would not have happened.*

> Ring *v.* Cohoes, 77 N. Y. 83.
> Merritt *v.* Fitzgibbons, 29 Hun, 634.
> (Rev. on other grounds, 102 N. Y. 362.)
> Wilson *v.* Atlanta, 60 Ga. 473.
> Williams *v.* D., L. & W. R. R. Co., 39 Hun, 430.
> Taylor *v.* Yonkers, 26 W. Dig. 376.

3. Application to city negligence cases. *When two causes combine to produce an injury to a traveller upon a highway,*

[106]

both of which are in their nature proximate, the one being a
culpable defect in a highway, and the other some occurrence for
which neither party is responsible, the municipality is liable,
provided the injury would not have been sustained but for such
defect.

> Macauley *r.* New York, 67 N. Y. 602.
> Kennedy *r.* New York, 73 N. Y. 365.
> Chicago *r.* Schmidt, 29 Alb. L. J. 479.
> Hampson *r.* Taylor, (R. I.) 32 Alb. L. J. 415.
> Bassett *v.* St. Joseph, 53 Mo. 290.
> Aldrich *r.* Gorham, 77 Me. 287.
> Clark *v.* Lebanon, 63 Me. 393.
> Galveston *r.* Posnainsky, 62 Tex. 118.
> Crawfordsville *r.* Smith, 79 Ind. 308.
> Lancaster *v.* Kissinger, (Pa.) 25 Alb. L. J. 454.

In Galveston *v.* Posnainsky, a child had fallen into an
excavation in the street, and was injured by broken glass
at the bottom. Held, that the excavation was the proximate cause.

In Chicago *r.* Schmidt, the plaintiff's intestate slipped
into a hole in a sidewalk, was thrown upon a railroad
track, his clothes caught upon a spike or nail in the sidewalk, which held him until a train ran over and killed
him. City held liable.

In Hampson *v.* Taylor, the plaintiff fell into a gully in
a street, upon which sleet had formed, but so recently
that no liability could be imputed to the city upon that
account alone. Held, that if the injury would not have
happened but for the gully the plaintiff might recover.

In Bassett *v.* St. Joseph, the plaintiff, in trying to avoid
the threatened kick of a mule, fell into a hole.

In Hull *v.* Kansas City, the reins caught under a horse's tail, causing the horse to back and fall into a hole in the road.

Illustrative of the converse of the above rule,—that the injury can be attributed to no cause not proximate,—is the case of

Merrill v. Portland, 4 Cliff. C. Ct. 138.

There a signboard attached to a projecting awning was struck by a wagon, and fell, hurting a passer by. Held, that the unsafe structure was not the proximate cause of the injury.

Some of the cases cited above will be noticed more fully in the next section.

4. **Runaway horses** While it is true that a municipal corporation is not liable for damages caused by runaway horses.

Ring v. Cohoes, 77 N. Y. 83.
Moss v. Burlington, 60 Iowa, 438.

and in some States even by statute; see

Perkins v. Fayette, 68 Maine, 152.
Titus v. Northbridge, 97 Mass. 258.
Houfe v. Fulton, 29 Wis. 296.

and the commissioners of highways in towns are not bound to make barriers strong enough to stop runaway horses,

Lane v. Wheeler, 35 Hun, 606.

(though a municipality should so guard by barriers, a dangerous place in a highway, that even skittish horses may be driven there,

Pittstown *v.* Hart, 89 Pa. St. 389.)

still it does not follow that there can be a recovery against a city in no case where a horse becomes frightened and runs away. On the contrary, whenever the injury would not have happened but for the defective condition of the street, there may be such recovery.

In Kennedy *v.* New York, 73 N. Y. 365, a horse suddenly became unmanageable and backed off a dock, with which it was the duty of the city to provide a string-piece, but that duty had been neglected. Held, error to dismiss the complaint; that the absence of the string-piece was the proximate cause.

Macauley *v.* New York, 67 N. Y. 602, was also a dock case; and, as in the Kennedy case, a horse was lost by becoming frightened and backing off. In this case, the dock was itself defective, there being a hole in it through which the horse saw the water below, at which it became frightened, backed against the string-piece, which was also out of repair and decayed, and which gave way. Held, that these defects were the proximate cause.

In Clark *v.* Lebanon, 63 Maine, 393, a well-broken horse, frightened at the carriage striking logs in the highway, ran away, and, at a distance of one hundred and twenty-five feet, threw out the driver, who was injured. Held, that the logs were the proximate cause.

In Aldrich *v.* Gorham, 77 Maine, 287, a well-broken horse shied and jumped upon a part of a bridge not usually travelled, and defective. Shying held not to be the proximate cause.

In Crawfordsville *v.* Smith, 79 Ind. 308, held that a plaintiff, using due care, might recover when his horse became frightened and ran into an excavation in a street.

CHAPTER XI.

DEGREE OF CARE.

1. Bound to reasonable care.
2. Not insurer.
3. Public works.
4. Individuals.
5. Active vigilance.
6. Care proportioned to danger.

1. Reasonable care. *It is the duty of a municipal corporation to keep its streets in a reasonably safe condition for public use ; and whether it does so or not is a question for the jury.*

> Hutson *v.* New York, 9 N. Y, 163.
> Todd *v.* Troy, 61 N. Y. 506.
> Clemence *v.* Auburn, 66 N. Y. 334.
> Evans *v.* Utica, 69 N. Y. 166.
> Niven *v.* Rochester, 76 N. Y. 619.
> Weed *v.* Ballston, Id. 329.
> Saulsbury *v.* Ithaca, 94 N. Y. 27.
> Dewire *v.* Bailey, 131 Mass. 169.

2. Not insurer. *A municipal corporation does not insure the absolutely safe condition of its streets. It is bound only to reasonable care and diligence for ordinary and reasonable use.*

> Ring *v.* Cohoes, 77 N. Y. 83.
> Stillwell *v.* New York, 49 Super. 360.
> Gorham *v.* Cooperstown, 59 N. Y. 660.

Battersby *r.* New York, 7 Daly, 16.
Muller *r.* Newburgh, 19 W. Dig. 550. 32 Hun, 24.
Wilson *r.* Granby, 47 Conn. 59.
Warren *r.* Wright, 3 Ill. Ap. 602.
Gibson *v.* Johnson, 4 Ill. Ap. 288.
Owen *v.* Chicago, 10 Ill. Ap. 465.
Rockford *r.* Hildebrand, 61 Ill. 155.
Chicago *v.* McGiven, 78 Ill. 347.
Kenyon *v.* Indianapalis, 1 Wilson (Ind.) 129.

In Kenyon *v.* Indianapolis, it is said that a city is liable only to remedy defects that may be detected and remedied by the use of ordinary care and diligence.

And in Stillwell *v.* New York, where the injury was caused by falling on a slippery vault cover, the court say : " The duty was to use ordinary care to furnish a reasonably safe place to step upon. There was no proof that in the performance of this duty the city could resort to any test but the appearance presented by the exterior of the cover."

In Chicago *v.* McGiven, it was held that a municipal corporation is not bound to furnish immunity, nor to use utmost care. That the street must be reasonably safe for persons using ordinary care and discretion.

In Muller *r.* Newburgh, an icy sidewalk case, the court say : " It is not practicable for municipal corporations to establish an incessant inspection of their streets; and without that it is impossible to guard against the conditions arising from natural causes. In our climate the streets and sidewalks are icy and slippery in winter, and their condition is produced by natural causes and does not depend on any care or skill in their construction or reparation."

See, also, **Taylor** *v.* **Yonkers**, 26 W. Dig. 376.

In Battersby *v.* New York : " To hold that the authorities must, under all circumstances and at all times, keep the streets clear of snow, ice or mud, would be unreasonable."

In Gorham *v.* Cooperstown it is said : "Municipal corporations are not guarantors for the absolute safety of all persons from injuries by reason of defects in or obstructions of the streets or highways of the municipality. They are only liable when the defects or obstructions are the results of their acts, or of some neglect or omission of duty by them or their servants or agents, and individuals in the use of streets receive injuries therefrom without fault on their part. Some overt act of the municipality or its officers, resulting in injury to third persons, or some neglect or omission of duty in repairing defects or removing obstructions, must be established, in order to charge the municipality with the consequences of any defects in or obstruction of thoroughfares within the corporation."

3. In construction of public works. The rule is similar, and has thus been stated :

A municipal corporation, in the construction of its sewers, drains, &c., is bound to exercise that care and prudence which a discreet and cautious individual would use if the loss or risk were to be his own.

> Rochester White Lead Co. *v.* Rochester, 3 N. Y. 463.
> New York *v.* Bailey, 2 Denio, 433.

4. Individuals. *Exactly the same rules apply, in this*

8

respect, to an individual or private corporation lawfully obstructing a street, or charged with a duty in respect to it.

> McMahon *v.* Second Ave. R. R. Co., 75 N. Y. 231.
> Nolan *v.* King, 97 N. Y. 565.
> Welsh *v.* Wilson, 101 N. Y. 254.
> Lanark Bank *v.* Eitemiller, 14 Ill. Ap. 22.

In Nolan *v.* King, a licensee who had removed the sidewalk, in order to construct a vault, built a bridge over the excavation, which bridge was necessarily higher than the street. It was held error on the part of the trial court to charge that it was the defendant's duty " to have the bridge constructed in such a manner that plaintiff would not be subjected to any more personal risk than if the sidewalk had been there instead of the bridge."

5. **Active vigilance.** *Where a municipal corporation is charged by its charter with the duty of keeping its streets in repair and in suitable condition for public travel, the agents of the corporation charged with that duty are bound to exercise an active vigilance in the performance thereof.*

> Todd *v.* Troy, 61 N. Y. 506.
> Atlanta *v.* Perdue, 53 Ga. 607.
> Rosenberg *v.* Des Moines, 41 Iowa, 415.
> Chicago *v.* Hoy, 75 Ill. 530.
> Pomfrey *v.* Saratoga Spr., 104 N. Y. 459.

6. **Care proportioned to danger.** The degree of care and foresight which it is necessary to use, must always be in proportion to the nature and magnitude of the injury that will be likely to result from the occurrence that is to be anticipated and provided against.

> New York *v.* Bailey, 2 Denio, 433.

In accordance with this principle, it has been often held that the more populous the thoroughfare the greater the degree of vigilance necessary on the part of the corporation.

Smid *v.* New York, 49 Super. 126.

For this reason only the care required in a village may not be equal to that in a city. There is no difference in principle.

Pomfrey *v.* Saratoga Spr., 5 N. Y. St. R. 802.

CHAPTER XII.

NOTICE.

1. Fact of obstruction not enough. *The mere fact that a street is obstructed or unsafe is not alone sufficient to charge a municipal corporation with negligence.*

> Griffin *v.* New York, 9 N. Y. 456.
> McGinity *v.* New York, 5 Duer, 674.
> Gorham *v.* Cooperstown, 59 N. Y. 660.
> Todd *v.* Troy, 61 N. Y. 506.
> Evans *v.* Utica, 69 N. Y. 166.
> Stanton *v.* Springfield, 12 Allen, 566.
> Cook *v.* Milwaukee, 24 Wis. 270.

Nor that an accident happened there.

> Baltimore El. Co. *v.* Neal, (Md.) 5 Atl. R. 338.

[116]

This principle is either expressed or implied in most of the cases cited in this chapter.

Some of the cases above cited and many others arose from injuries caused by falls upon icy sidewalks.

Thus, in Todd *v.* Troy, it was held that the mere fact of ice upon a sidewalk upon which the plaintiff slipped and fell, did not establish the liability of the city.

2. Obstructions caused by city or agents. *Where, however, the obstruction is caused by the city itself, the above rule does not apply. In such cases no notice need be proven, the presumption being that every one has knowledge of his own acts.*

> Brusso *v.* Buffalo, 90 N. Y. 679.
> Platz *v.* Cohoes, 89 N. Y. 219.
> Groves *v.* Rochester, 39 Hun, 5.
> Sevestre *v.* New York, 47 Super. 341.
> Holmes *v.* Paris, 75 Maine, 559.
> Brunswick *v.* Braxton, 70 Ga. 193.
> Alexander *v.* Mt. Sterling, 71 Ill. 366.

And the fact that the work was done through a contractor does not vary the rule.

> Brusso *v.* Buffalo, *supra.*

In Brunswick *v.* Braxton, the obstruction was made by an "agent"; in Holmes *v.* Paris, by a "servant"; in Groves *v.* Rochester, by an "executive board."

The above rule applies where the work was done by private persons, *under the supervision* of the city authorities.

> Wendell *v.* Troy, 4 Abb. Dec. 563.

But some question has arisen as to just what constitutes supervision.

3. License not notice. *The fact that an obstruction is made in the course of work done in pursuance of a resolution or ordinance of a municipal corporation, or by its licensee, does not necessarily make it the act of the city, so as to make notice unnecessary.*

> Masterton *v.* Mount Vernon, 58 N. Y. 391.
> Sweet *v.* Gloversville, 12 Hun, 302.
> Dorlon *v.* Brooklyn, 46 Barb. 604.
> McDermott *v.* Kingston, 19 Hun. 198.
> Cohen *v.* New York, 43 Hun, 345.

In Sweet *v.* Gloversville, the excavation was made by a contractor with a person who by resolution of the trustees of the village had been directed to lower his sidewalk.

In Dorlon *v.* Brooklyn, the city had granted a license to a plumber employed by private persons to connect a house with a city sewer. The injury was caused by the plumber's negligence.

In McDermott *v.* Kingston, the excavation was made by a gas company, acting under a license granted by ordinance.

In all these cases it was held that the city could not be charged without notice shown.

4. Need of notice, generally. This brings us to the general rule upon the subject of notice :

A municipal corporation is not liable for injuries caused to individuals by obstructions on the highway, not placed there by its own officials or by authority of the city government, until after actual notice of their existence, or until, by reason of the lapse of time, it should have had knowledge, and therefore actual notice may be presumed.

Hume *v.* New York, 47 N. Y. 639.
Griffin *v.* New York, 9 N. Y. 456.
McGinity *v.* New York, 5 Duer, 674.
Hart *v.* Brooklyn, 36 Barb. 226.
Dorlon *v.* Brooklyn, 46 Barb. 604.
Masterson *v.* Mt. Vernon, 58 N. Y. 391.
Smith *v.* New York, 66 N. Y. 295.
Weed *v.* Ballston, 76 N. Y. 329.
McKenna *v.* New York, 47 Super. 541.
Hunt *v.* New York, 52 Id. 198.
Rehberg *v.* New York, 91 N. Y. 137.
Ehrgott *v.* New York, 96 N. Y. 264.
Herrington *v.* Phœnix, 41 Hun, 270.
Chicago *v.* McCarthy, 75 Ill. 602.
Schweickhardt *v.* St. Louis, 2 Mo. Ap. 571.
Mack *v.* Salem, 6 Oregon, 275.

That the notice may be either actual or constructive, and the distinction between these two terms, cannot be better stated than in the above rule.

5. Ignorance itself negligence. *The rule that a municipal corporation must have notice, has no application where its ignorance of the defect is the result of a clear and unmistakable omission.*

Boucher *v.* New Haven, 40 Conn. 456.

6. Actual notice; to whom? As a city can act only through its agents and officers, it follows that notice of the condition of its streets can be given only to them.

A question then arises as to who are to be regarded as agents or officers, by whose knowledge of an obstruction a municipal corporation will be bound.

In the following cases, notice to the officers named was held to bind the corporation.

Mayor or marshal.

> Salina *v.* Trosper, 27 Kans. 544.

Councilman.

> Logansport *v.* Justice, 74 Ind. 378.

Superintendent of streets.

> Deyoe *v.* Saratoga, 3 T. & C. 504.

Street commissioner.

> Childs *v.* West Troy, 23 Hun, 68.
> Welch *v.* Portland, (Me.) 1 East. R. 586.

Policeman.

> Rehberg *v.* New York, 91 N. Y. 137.
> Twogood *v.* New York, 102 N. Y. 216.

In the last case, evidence was given that a patrolman whose duty it was to report violations of ordinances to his superior officer reported snow and ice not removed on the spot where the plaintiff fell, for seven successive days before the injury. The trial court held that these reports did not constitute notice to the city. The general term affirmed, but the court of appeals reversed the judgment.

In the following cases it was held that the city was not chargeable with notice :

One alderman.

> Peach *v.* Utica, 10 Hun, 477.
> McDermott *v.* Kingston, 19 Hun, 198.

In the former case the court say : "I am not prepared to say that notice to the common council of a defect in a street or walk may not be proved by showing that it was known to a considerable number of aldermen."

In both cases it was held that evidence of notice to one alderman was admissible as a link in the chain of proof, and should not be neglected as wholly incompetent.

In Huggins *v.* Salamanca, 25 W. Dig. 401, where several of the trustees knew of the excavation and gave directions concerning it, it was held proper for the jury to determine the question of notice.

Two trustees.

> Bush *v.* Geneva, 3 T. & C. 409.

Lamplighter, where the charter did not require lamps.

> Monies *v.* Lynn, 119 Mass. 273.

Janitor, appointed by school committee.

> Foster *v.* Boston, 127 Mass. 290.

7. **Constructive notice sufficient.** That it is not necessary in all cases to show actual notice to a city or its agents of the defective condition of its streets, has already been stated, and is too well established for comment to be necessary. Among the many cases holding that constructive notice is enough are the following :

122   LAW.

Walker *r.* Lockhart, 43 How. Pr. 366.
Weed *v.* Ballston, 76 N. Y. 329.
Requa *r.* Rochester, 45 N. Y. 129.
Diveny *v.* Elmira, 51 N. Y. 506.
Hume *r.* New York, 47 N. Y. 639.
Pettengill *v.* Yonkers, 23 W. Dig. 333.
Porter Co. Comrs. *v.* Dombke, 94 Ind. 72.
Dotton *r.* Albion Com. Council, 50 Mich. 129.
Chicago *v.* Dalle, 115 Ill. 386.
Goodfellow *v.* New York, 100 N. Y. 15,

8. Constructive notice, from what inferred. The elements
of constructive notice to a municipal corporation may be
discovered in the following decisions.

In Indianapolis *v.* Murphy, 91 Ind. 382, it is said that
such knowledge is inferable from length of time, considered with reference to the facts and circumstances of
the particular case.

In Shook *v.* Cohoes, 23 W. Dig. 4, that besides time,
the elements are position, character, and cause of defect.

In Requa *v.* Rochester, 45 N. Y. 129, that sufficient
time must have elapsed to render the defect notorious.

In Chicago *v.* Fowler, 60 Ill. 322, that where the jury
believe the defect or obstruction has been so long and
so notorious that the city should have known its existence and provided protection, they may find the city
liable.

In Dotton *r.* Albion, 50 Mich. 129, that notice may be
presumed from the existence of facts with which ignorance would be incompatible unless failure to exercise
reasonable care be assumed.

In Todd *v.* Troy, 61 N. Y. 506, the court say: "By constructive notice is meant such notice as the law imputes from the circumstances of the case. It is the duty of the municipal authorities to exercise an active vigilance over the streets; to see that they are kept in a reasonably safe condition for public travel. They cannot fold their arms and shut their eyes, and say they have no notice. After a street has been out of repair so that the defect has become known and notorious to those travelling the street, and there has been full opportunity for the municipality, through its agents charged with that duty, to learn of its existence and repair it, the law imputes to it notice and charges it with negligence," and cite the following cases:

> Hart *r.* Brooklyn, 36 Barb. 226.
> Clark *r.* Lockport, 49 Barb. 580.
> Conrad *v.* Ithaca, 16 N. Y. 158.
> Requa *r.* Rochester, *supra.*
> Hyatt *r.* Rondout, 44 Barb. 385.

In Albrittin *v.* Huntsville, 60 Ala. 486, it was held that the fact that a defect in a sidewalk had existed long enough to be within the observation of people generally, raises the presumption that the authorities knew it.

In Hearn *v.* Chicago, 20 Bradwell (Ill.) 251, it is held that "it is not necessary, in order to charge the city with implied notice of a defect in a sidewalk, that the circumstances should be such as to charge the particular person or persons having special supervision of the sidewalks with such notice. It is enough if the circumstances raise an implication of notice to any officer or agent of the city, whose duty it is to communicate to the city or its proper executive officers the existence of such defect."

9. Length of time to constitute constructive notice. **Question for whom ?** (a) *General rule.* Upon this point there are two lines of authorities. The general rule is that it is purely a question of fact for the jury.

> Chicago *v.* McCulloch, 10 Ill. Ap. 459.
> Sheel *v.* Appleton, 49 Wis. 125.
> Rehberg *v.* New York, 91 N. Y. 137.
> Kunz *v.* Troy, 35 Alb. L. J. 232 ; 5 N. Y. St. R. 642.
> Reed *v.* New York, 31 Hun, 311.
> Kinney *v.* Troy, 38 Hun, 285.

In Chicago *v.* McCulloch, held that no length of notice can be fixed as matter of law, after which a city will be bound for failure to remove an obstacle.

In Sheel *v.* Appleton, that it is purely a question for the jury; that one day may be enough.

In Reed *v.* New York, the court say that "reasonable time" is for the jury to determine, and that a refusal to so charge was error.

(b) *Obstruction by elements.* In several cases where the injury has been caused by falling upon icy sidewalks, a non-suit has been held proper upon the ground of insufficient notice to charge the corporation.

Such cases are :

> Muller *v.* Newburgh, 32 Hun, 24.
> Garrett *v.* Buffalo, 22 W. Dig. 262.
> Smith *v.* Brooklyn, 86 Hun, 224.
> Heintze *v.* New York, 50 Super. 295.
> Evers *v.* Hudson River Br. Co., 18 Hun, 144.
> Blakely *v.* Troy, 18 Hun, 167.

The grounds on which these cases are decided is summarized in two Massachusetts cases, as follows :

If the obstruction be produced by the elements, liability will not attach to the corporation unless neglect on his part is shown, after knowledge or notice of the obstruction and a reasonable time for its removal.

> Billings v. Worcester, 102 Mass. 329.
> Street v. Holyoke, 105 Mass. 82.

In Muller v. Newburgh, the plaintiff fell Sunday evening. Snow had fallen the Thursday before, after which it rained and the rain had frozen hard. It was "a case where the snow first came down on the sidewalk and was softened by the rain, and then the whole mass was congealed and hardened as it lay, and while a light snow was yet falling on this surface of ice, the plaintiff slipped and received this injury." The court say:

"It is not practicable for the municipal corporations of this State to establish an incessant inspection of their streets, and without that it is impossible to guard against the conditions arising from natural causes. In our latitude climatic changes are frequent and sudden. Ice and snow may dissolve into water during the day, even in winter, and spread over the sidewalk and harden to ice in the night, or the pavements may become slippery from moisture or rain, and both these causes may produce accidents and injuries which no extent of vigilance and care would prevent, and which the corporation cannot be called on to redress."

In Smith v. Brooklyn, snow fell November 28th and

29th, which subsequently melted and ice formed therefrom. The plaintiff fell December 4th. The court say:

"In our climate no reasonable amount of care can
prevent the accumulation of ice and snow, and all that is
required from municipal corporations is reasonable care
and diligence. And what is reasonable must be determined in view of all the surrounding conditions. Our
seasons are fluctuating, the inspection of streets is not
incessant, the officers and means provided for that purpose are limited, and after the exertion of all reasonable
diligence defects and obstructions will exist and injuries
will result."

In Evers v. Hudson River Br. Co., the plaintiff fell
between 8 and 9 o'clock in the morning upon ice which
had formed by the freezing of rain which had fallen
during the night.

In Blakely v. Troy, ice formed during the night, and
plaintiff fell at one o'clock the next afternoon.

In that case it appeared, however, that there was ice
there before, and upon appeal it was held that in such
case the city might still be liable.

In Kenney v. Cohoes, 16 W. Dig. 206, on the other
hand, it appeared that rain fell during the night and
froze before morning at the place where the plaintiff fell.
There was, however, a prior accumulation of ice. It was
held not error to refuse to charge that if the walk had
not been slippery before the new ice formed, the plaintiff
could not recover, since it might be inferred that the rain
washed dirt from the old ice, thus rendering it slippery.

In Garrett *v.* Buffalo, ice formed on a slanting drive-way, without negligence of the city. The walk was cleaned the day before, and rain fell and froze in the night.

Of this class of cases the court say, in Kinney *v.* Troy, 38 Hun, 285 :

"In Muller *v.* Newburgh, 32 Hun, 24, a majority of the court held that when ice formed on Thursday and the plaintiff fell and was injured on Sunday, there was not evidence for the jury on the question of presumptive notice to the defendant. I think great difficulty will be found, if the courts attempt to declare, as law, what time the obstruction must have existed in order to permit the question of notice to go to the jury."

(c) For the purpose of avoiding the difficulty of establishing notice, it is often desirable to establish something more than the mere continued existence of ice.

In some cases it has been made to appear that the accident occurred by reason of ice forming upon improperly constructed or uneven sidewalks.

Urquhart *r.* Ogdensburgh, 97 N. Y. 238.
Atchison *r.* King, 9 Kan. 553.
Mauch Chunk *v.* Kline, 100 Pa. St. 119.

In others, that the water which formed the ice was conducted to the street or sidewalk by artificial means—as hydrants, leaders from roofs, &c.—of the existence of

which, and of the tendency to form ice, the city had or
ought to have had notice.

> Mosey v. Troy, 61 Barb. 580.
> (S. C. in court of appeals) Todd v. Troy, 61 N. Y.
>   506.
> Dempsey v. New York, 10 Daly, 417.
> Reich v. New York, 12 Daly, 72.
> Darling v. New York, 18 Hun, 340.
> Allison v. Middletown, 23 W. Dig. 149 ; 101 N. Y.
>   667.
> Powers v. Chicago, 20 Bradw. (Ill.) 178.

10. Latent defects. *The law does not presume notice to a
municipal corporation of latent defects.*

> Scanlon v. New York, 12 Daly, 81.
> Hunt v. New York, 52 Super. 198.
> Hart v. Brooklyn, 36 Barb. 226.
> Hanscom v. Boston, 33 Alb. L. J. 355.
> Joliet v. Walker, 7 Ill. Ap. 267.

In Hunt v. New York, the injury was caused by an
explosion resulting from the ignition of gas which had
accumulated and filled a man-hole constructed and
owned by a private corporation.

In Hart v. Brooklyn, it was caused by the slipping of
a vault grating when the plaintiff stepped upon it.

In Joliet v. Walker the court say: "A municipal
corporation will not be considered to have notice of a
defect in a sidewalk which was not such as to put a reasonable, prudent man, whose business it was to look after
the repairs, on inquiry to examine its condition.

11. Duty of city. *The above rule is, however, subject to the
duty of the city to use ordinary caution to anticipate the dan-*

*ger that could come into existence without manifesting itself to
ordinary observation.*

Vosper r. New York, 49 Super. 296.

Or as otherwise stated :

" The duty of keeping a highway in order involves
the duty of reasonable supervision. And when exercise
of such supervision would have led to the discovery of a
defect in season to repair it, or protect the public against
it, there is the same liability as though there had been
actual knowledge."

Cusick v. Norwich, 40 Conn. 375.
Kunz r. Troy, 5 N. Y. St. R. 642. 104 N. Y. 344.
Market r. St. Louis, 56 Mo. 189.
Weed v. Ballston, 76 N. Y. 329.

In Vosper *v.* New York the injury was caused by the
falling of a tree standing on the sidewalk, which, after its
fall, was found to be rotten to a dangerous degree from
its roots up.

It was held that the duty of the city is not limited to
acting upon exterior signs of danger, and that it was a
question for the jury to determine whether or not the
defendants should by some means have anticipated the
danger, even by cutting down the tree.

The case of Gubasco *v.* New York, 12 Daly, 192, was
similar, the injury being caused by the throwing down,
by a passing truck, of a tree which had been dead several
years, and had a large hole, but the evidence of its rot-
tenness was conflicting.

In Indianapolis *v.* Scott, 72 Ind. 196, it was held that

9

a city is chargeable with knowledge of the tendency of timber to rot by lapse of time and exposure to weather.

12. Statute fixing notice constitutional. The liability of the city of Schenectady for injuries caused by the dangerous condition of its streets, is by statute conditioned upon twenty-four hours' notice, previous to the injury, to the common council or superintendent of its streets.

Held, constitutional in

Van Vranken *v.* Schenectady, 31 Hun, 516.

12. Particular defect. In Weisenberg *v.* Appleton, 26 Wis. 56, held that a city may be liable for a sidewalk in an unsound and dangerous condition, if the authorities did not know the particular defect existed.

13. No presumption from ownership. In Heintze *v.* New York, 50 Super. 295, held that the fact of ownership by the city of premises to which a dangerous sidewalk is adjacent, raises no presumption of notice.

Here may be noticed, Lowhouse *v.* Buffalo, 22 W. Dig, 49, that ownership by the State of arsenal property within a city does not excuse the city from the duty of keeping the street safe for travellers.

CHAPTER XIII.

CONTRIBUTORY NEGLIGENCE.

1. General rule. The principle of contributory negligence is well stated in the following :

An action for negligence cannot be sustained if the wrongful act or negligence of the plaintiff co-operated with the misconduct of the defendant, to produce the injury complained of.

Munger *v.* Tonawanda R. R. Co., 4 N. Y. 349.
Monongahela *v.* Fischer, (Penn.) 3 East. R. 095.

It is useless to multiply authorities upon this well-known principle. Their number is legion.

[131]

2. Proximate cause. *Though the plaintiff were negligent, yet if his negligence did not contribute to the injury; or, in other words, if, notwithstanding his negligence, the injury would still have happened, the contributory negligence will not bar recovery.*

> Haley v. Earle, 30 N. Y. 208.
> Van Ostran v. N. Y. C. &c. R. R. Co., 35 Hun, 590.
> Kline v. C. P. R. R. Co., 37 Cal. 400.
> Needham v. San Francisco R. R. Co., Id. 400.
> Flynn v. San Francisco, &c. R. R. Co., 40 Cal. 14.
> Rome v. Dodd, 58 Ga. 238.
> Centerville v. Woods, 57 Ind. 192.
> Pacific R. R. Co. v. Houts, 12 Kan. 328.
> Mississippi Cent. R. R. Co. v. Mason, 51 Miss. 234.
> Walsh v. Mississippi, &c. Co., 52 Mo. 434.
> Frick v. St. Louis, &c. Ry. Co., 5 Mo. Ap. 435.
> New Jersey Exp. Co. v. Nichols, 33 N. J. L. 434.
> Hurst v. Burnside, (Or.) 8 Pac. R. 888.
> Gould v. McKenna, 86 Pa. St. 297.

3. Degree of care. *There is no contributory negligence when the injured party acts with ordinary prudence, on that apprehension of danger which he is bound to have under the circumstances, and those appearances of danger which the situation manifests.*

> Nowell v. New York, 52 Super. 382.

That ordinary care only is required to avert the charge of contributory negligence, is held also in

> Center v. Finney, 17 Barb. 94 ; Seld. N. 80.
> Eakin v. Brown, 1 E. D. Smith, 36.
> Lancaster v. Kissinger, (Pa.) 25 Alb. L. J. 454.
> Dupree v. Cent. Pac. Ry. Co., 7 Pac. R. 953.
> Wooley v. Grand St., &c. R. R. Co., 83 N. Y. 121.

In Center v. Finney the court say :

"If ordinary diligence by the plaintiff will not prevent the injury, he is not considered in any degree the author of the wrong."

In Wooley *v.* Grand St., &c. Co., the injury was caused by a sleigh being overturned by a switch laid on the street by a licensed company. The court say:

"It is incumbent upon the owner of the special franchise to use a switch put down in a manner that is consonant with the general rightful use of the same public way. That general rightful use is such use as men of ordinary care and prudence, having knowledge of the location of the switch, will exercise when passing over that part of the public way, at which the switch is laid down. The citizen is bound to expect to meet such fixtures in the use of his common right of travel over the street, and is bound to use that care in approaching and passing by or over it, on foot or in vehicles, that men of ordinary care and prudence would put forth in the same locality and circumstances."

In Lancaster *v.* Kissinger the plaintiff, seated on one of a load of loose boxes in a wagon, was thrown off in crossing a gutter. The court say:

"What was the proper measure of care under such circumstances? The same care that a man with a fixed load and a firm seat would be expected to take? Certainly not. Negligence is the absence of care according to the circumstances. If a man is driving an untamed horse he naturally and properly exercises more care than if he were driving one entirely gentle: so of the road, if

it is rough and out of repair he exercises more care than
if well graded and macadamized."

The converse of the rule given at the head of this
section is thus stated :

" *If in the use of ordinary care and prudence such as the
ordinarily prudent person would have used under the same
circumstances, it [the defect] ought to have been discovered,
then the plaintiff cannot recover.*"

Minick v. Troy, 83 N. Y. 514.

In accordance with these principles it has been held
that a charge that the plaintiff cannot recover if guilty of
"any negligence whatever" is erroneous, as implying that
extreme care is required of the traveller.

And on the other hand, that it is not error to refuse to
charge that the plaintiff is bound to use extraordinary
care when a sidewalk is slippery ; and a charge that there
is demanded "reasonable care in view of this fact" was
held proper.

Monahan v. Cohoes, 14 W. Dig. 112.

4. Cases. Recovery barred. Illustrative of the last
section are the following cases, in each of which it was
held that the plaintiff's own negligence prevented his
recovery.

(a) Walking on an embankment thrown up while
excavation being made—street wide enough to pass.

Carolus v. New York, 6 Bosw. 15.

(b) Walking on ice in daytime—plenty of space either side for passing.

Quincy v. Barker, 81 Ill. 300.

(c) Walking hastily or negligently, or knowing of defect and able to have avoided it by taking the other side of the street.

Lovenguth v. Bloomington, 71 Ill. 238.

(d) Walking in an absent-minded, inattentive, negligent manner, and so stumbling over an obstruction which a prudent person could have avoided.

Chicago v. Bixby, 84 Ill. 82.
Vicksburgh v. Hennessey, 54 Miss. 391.

(e) Stepping deliberately from sidewalk, with sufficient light and good eyesight, into a pitfall beside the walk.

Monmouth v. Sullivan, 8 Ill. Ap. 50.
McLaury v. McGregor, 54 Iowa, 717.

(f) To descend a stair-case known to be slippery, failing to use a hand-rail.

Foster v. New York Central, &c. R. R. Co., 2 How.
Pr. N. S. 416; 23 W. Dig. 18.

(g) Stepping into opening on sidewalk, lighted by a lamp immediately over opening—sidewalk of usual width and opening close to house for light and ventilation.

King v. Thompson, 87 Pa. St. 365.

(h)   Where a street opposite a building in process of erection is so encroached upon by piles of rubbish that only sufficient room is left for one vehicle to pass—attempting in daylight to pass another carriage by driving over the obstruction.

Griffin v. New York, 9 N. Y. 456.

(i)   Stranger in city, on dark night, voluntarily left his companion who was familiar with the locality and had a lantern, and walked through an opening in a bridge.

Cummins v. Syracuse, 3 East. Rep. 198.
[Mem.] 100 N. Y. 637.

(j)   Running to fire, fell over stepping-stone on wide sidewalk, in front of lighted post-office, gas-light beside stone.

Dubois v. Kingston, 102 N. Y. 219.

5. Presumption of safety.   *The ordinary diligence required of a city in the care of its streets is by no means the measure of the ordinary diligence required of a traveller upon those streets.*

Wilson v. Atlanta, 63 Ga. 291.

The city is charged with a duty to keep its streets in order, and, it may almost be said, is bound to act upon the assumption that they are unsafe.

On the contrary : " All persons using streets and sidewalks have the right to assume that they are in good and safe condition, and to regulate their conduct upon that assumption."

Kenyon v. Indianapolis, 1 Wilson (Ind.) 139.

" Any person travelling a sidewalk of a city, which is in constant use by the public, has a right, when using the same with due diligence, to presume, and act upon the presumption, that it is reasonably safe for ordinary travel, throughout its entire width, from all dangers and annoying obstructions of a permanent character."

Indianapolis v. Gaston, 58 Ind. 224.

" A person passing along a sidewalk has a right to presume it to be safe, and is bound to no special care ; and is not bound to watch for unlawful obstructions."

Dorland v. N. Y. C. & H. R. R. R. Co., 19 W. Dig. 76.

" One who passes along a sidewalk has a right to presume it to be safe. He is not called upon to anticipate danger, and is not negligent for not being on his guard."

McGuire v. Spence, 91 N. Y. 303.

" A person travelling on a public street, if he exercises ordinary care, has a right to be absolutely safe against all accidents arising from obstructions or imperfections in the streets."

Lincoln v. Walker, (Neb.) 30 Alb. L. J. 406.
Chicago v. Hickok, 17 Bradw. (Ill.) 142.

" The streets and sidewalks are for the benefit of all conditions of people, and all have the right, in using them, to assume that they are in good condition, and to regulate their conduct upon that assumption. A person may walk or drive in the darkness of the night, relying upon the belief that the corporation has performed its duty and that the street or the walk is in a safe condition.

He walks by a faith justified by law, and if his faith is unfounded and he suffers an injury, the party in fault must respond in damages."

Davenport v. Ruckman, 37 N. Y. 568.

This principle is, however, subject to the rule that: "Persons walking in a city are bound to take notice of the existence of such constructions as the necessities of commerce and the convenient occupation of residences render common."

(For instance, exterior basement stairs.)

Buesching v. St. Louis Gas Light Co., 6 Mo. Ap. 85.

It should also be observed that the ordinary care required of a traveller upon the highway is not the same as that of one about to cross a railroad track, "where there is reason to expect danger, and where the person crossing must be on the look-out."

Childs v. West Troy, 23 Hun, 68.
Gumb v. Twenty-third St. R. R. Co., 1 N. Y. St. R. 715.

6. Right to whole street. *One not only has a perfect right to walk across a street, and being in a public thoroughfare has a right to assume that his rights will not be wrongfully invaded,*

Moody v. Osgood, 54 N. Y. 488.

But is not obliged to go upon a cross-walk. He has a right to assume the whole street to be reasonably safe.

Brusso v. Buffalo, 90 N. Y. 679.
Raymond v. Lowell, 6 Cush. 524.

Knight *r.* Bath-on-the Hudson, 21 W. Dig. 30?.
Simons *r.* Gaynor, 89 Ind. 165.

To walk upon the carriage-way of a bridge, though it have a sidewalk, is not *per se* negligent.

Morrell *v.* Peck, 88 N. Y. 398.

7. Knowledge of defect. *That the person injured knew of the defect or obstruction before the injury does not per se establish negligence on his part.*

Diveny *r.* Elmira, 51 N. Y. 506.
Todd *r.* Troy, 61 Id. 506.
Evans *v.* Utica, 69 Id. 166.
Bassett *r.* Fish, 75 Id. 303.
Weed *r.* Ballston, 76 Id. 329.
Palmer *v.* Dearing, 93 Id. 7.
Bullock *r.* New York, 99 Id. 654.
Twogood *r.* New York, 102 Id. 216.
Driscoll *r.* New York, 11 Hun, 101.
Koch *r.* Edgewater, 14 Id. 544.
Darling *v.* New York, 18 Id. 340.
Harris *v.* Perry, 23 Id. 244 ; rev'd on other grounds,
      89 N. Y. 308.
Thomas *v.* New York, 28 Id. 110.
Pomfrey *v.* Saratoga, 34 Id. 607.
Bateman *v.* Ruth, 3 Daly, 378.
Vandercook *v.* Cohoes, 12 W. Dig. 84.
Dunham *v.* Canandaigua, 13 Id. 551.
Gage *r.* Hornellsville, 24 Id. 276.
Phillips *r.* Fishkill, 26 Id. 103.
Montgomery *v.* Wright, 72 Ala. 411.
Bronson *r.* Smithbury, 37 Conn. 199.
Aurora *r.* Dale, 90 Ill. 46.
Huntington *r.* Breen, 77 Ind. 29.
Madison Co. Comrs. *r.* Brown, 89 Id. 48.
Albion *v.* Herrick, 90 Id. 545.
Wilson *r.* Trafalgar, &c. Gravel Road Co., 93 Id. 287.
Jeffrey *r.* Keokuk, &c. Ry. Co., 56 Iowa, 546.
Osage City *r.* Brown, 27 Kan. 74.
Maultby v. Leavenworth, 28 Id. 745.

Emporia v. Scheindling, 33 Id. 485.
Langan v. Atchinson, (Kan.) 11 Pac. R. 38.
Prince George's Co. Comrs. v. Burgess, 61 Md. 29.
Dewire v. Bailey, 131 Mass. 169.
Gilbert v. Boston, 139 Id. 313.
Lowell v. Watertown, (Mich.) 33 Alb. L. J. 19.
Estelle v. Lake Crystal, 27 Minn. 243.
McKenzie v. Northfield, 30 Id. 456.
Hubbard v. Concord, 35 N. H. 52.
Templeton v. Montpelier, (Vt.) 30 Alb. L. J. 358.
Kavanaugh v. Janesville, 24 Wis. 618.
Kenworthy v. Ironton, 41 Wis. 647.

The rule is that he must use the ordinary care and prudence which the circumstances demand.

Diveny v. Elmira, *supra*.
Palmer v. Dearing, *supra*.
Bullock v. New York, *supra*.
Koch v. Edgewater, *supra*.
Huntington v. Breen, *supra*.
Wilson v. Trafalgar, &c. Co., *supra*.
Joliet v. Conway, 17 Bradw. (Ill.) 577.

And recovery will not be prevented unless a person of ordinary prudence would not have walked there.

McKenzie v. Northfield, *supra*.
Evans v. Utica, *supra*.

And it is ordinarily a question for the jury.

Bullock v. New York, *supra*.
Pomfrey v. Saratoga, *supra*.
Driscoll v. New York, *supra*.
Twogood v. New York, *supra*.
Todd v. Troy, *supra*.
Brusso v. Buffalo, 90 N. Y. 679.
McGuire v. Spence, 99 N. Y. 654.

(a) It has been held in different cases, that a person under such circumstances may be excused,

If his attention was not called to the obstruction at the time of the injury,

> Darling *r.* New York, *supra*.
> Thomas *v.* New York, *supra*.

or if he believed it to be reasonably safe, and there was no other walk convenient,

> Montgomery *r.* Wright, *supra*.
> Albion *r.* Herrick, *supra*.

or, though watching for the defect in order to avoid it, was prevented from doing so by a blinding snow-storm ; and other sidewalks leading to his home were equally unsafe.

> Aurora *r.* Dale, *supra*.

In Jeffrey *v.* Keokuk, &c. Ry. Co., *supra*, held that a person may voluntarily and without actual necessity expose himself to danger and yet recover.

In Osage City *v.* Brown, *supra*, that an old man walking rapidly in a dark night, and being injured upon an obstruction of which he knew, might recover.

So in Twogood *v.* New York, *supra*, though the walk were icy and the other walk clear.

And in Driscoll *v.* New York, *supra*, though the plaintiff failed to pay attention to a hole which had existed for several years at a street corner near her house, on account of her mind being engrossed in business.

(b) The following cases are selected in which it was held that the contributory negligence of the plaintiff prevented a recovery.

Plaintiff voluntarily attempted to pass over a sidewalk of a city, which he knew to be dangerous by reason of ice upon it, which he might easily have avoided.

Schaefler v. Sandusky, 33 Ohio St. 246.

Shown to have passed over same slippery sidewalk an hour before.

Macomb v. Smithers, 6 Ill. Ap. 470.

Attempted in the dark to pass an open cellar-way in a sidewalk, knowing, but for the time forgetting its existence.

Bruker v. Covington, 69 Ind. 33.

Voluntarily left safe, well-lighted sidewalk and fell into a hole eight feet away.

Zettler v. Atlanta, 66 Ga. 195.

Cautioned by his wife just before stepping on the ice.

Durkin v. Troy, 61 Barb. 437.

Knew walk was unsafe and there was another on which she might have passed safely.

Parkhill v. Brighton, 61 Iowa, 103.

Attempted in night-time to cross excavation with which he was familiar, on planks, instead of going around.

Momence v. Kendall, 14 Ill. Ap. 229.

Knowing of the existence of ice upon the sidewalk,

took the risk of walking there rather than the inconvenience of turning out into the street.

Erie v. Magill, 101 Pa. St. 616.

Or of going around through an alley.

Fleming v. Lockhaven, (Pa.) 31 A. L. J. 178.

(c) All the above cases should be considered in connection with the following general rule :

Where one, knowing the defective condition of a sidewalk, ventures upon it without taking the precaution necessary to prevent a fall, he cannot recover.

Aurora v. Brown, 11 Ill. Ap. 122.
Mayhew v. Burns, (Ind.) 2 No. East. R. 793.
Erie v. Magill, 101 Pa. St. 616.
Schaefler v. Sandusky, 33 Ohio St. 246.
Wilson v. Charlestown, 8 Allen, 137.
Parkhill v. Brighton, 61 Iowa, 103.
Cook v. Johnson, 58 Mich. 437.

8. **Latent defects.** *A traveller is by no means required to avoid defects or obstructions which he cannot see.*

Clark v. Lockport, 49 Barb. 580.
Van Alstine v. Clyde, 17 W. Dig. 565.

In the former case, an icy sidewalk was covered with snow; in the latter, the defect in a plank walk was in the string-pieces and out of sight.

9. Defective vision. *For a person with defective sight to walk the streets of a city is not* per se *negligent.*

> Davenport *v.* Ruckman, 37 N. Y. 568.
> Requa *v.* Rochester, 45 N. Y. 129.
> Peach *v.* Utica, 10 Hun, 477.
> Harris *v.* Uebelhoer, 75 N. Y. 169.

In the first three cases, the plaintiff was partially blind, and unattended; in the last case, totally blind and attended by his wife.

In Davenport *v.* Ruckman the court say :

" One whose sight is dimmed by age, or a near-sighted person whose range of vision was always imperfect, or one whose sight has been injured by disease, is each entitled to the same rights, and may act upon the same assumption."

So, too, to drive a partly blind horse has been held not of necessity negligence.

> Wright *v.* Templeton, 132 Mass. 49.

10. Intoxication. (a) *Intoxication is not* per se *contributory negligence. It does not preclude recovery, unless it contributed thereto, and that is a question for the jury.*

> Healy *v.* New York, 6 T. & C. 92 ; 3 Hun, 708.
> Ditchett *v.* Spuyten Duyvil, &c. R. R. Co., 5 Hun, 162.
> (Rev'd on other grounds, 67 N. Y. 425.)

In other words, a plaintiff is not debarred from recovery by reason of intoxication, unless he was thereby disabled from the exercise of ordinary care.

> O'Hagan *v.* Dillon, 42 Super. 456.
> (Rev'd on other grounds, 76 N. Y. 170.)

But if proper precaution were thereby prevented he cannot recover.

Illinois Central R. R. Co. *v.* Cragin, 71 Ill. 177.
Cramer *v.* Burlington, 42 Iowa, 315.
Monk *v.* New Utrecht, 104 N. Y. 561.

In Wood *v.* Andes, 11 Hun, 543, a man much intoxicated, and after having been warned against it, attempted to cross an unsafe bridge, and fell and was killed; no recovery.

(b)   *On the other hand, the fact of intoxication cannot avail to excuse contributory negligence.*

Illinois Cent. R. R. Co. *v.* Hutchinson, 47 Ill. 408.

11 Infant. In case a child of immature years sustains injury by the negligence of another, and an action is brought, either in its own behalf or in behalf of its parents or other persons entitled, the question of contributory negligence is more complicated than in the case of an adult.

(a)   *The contributory negligence, if any, may be that of the infant itself, or its parent or the person entrusted with its care.*

Whether or not negligence may be imputed to the infant itself depends upon whether or not it is of such tender age as to be not responsible for its acts.

Mangam *v.* Brooklyn R. R. Co., 38 N. Y. 455.

If the child is *sui juris*, and negligent, or if *non sui juris* and contributed by its acts to the injury, and the acts of

10

the parent also contributed to the injury, then there can
be no recovery.

(b) *Unless the child did, or omitted to do, something which
would have been negligence in an adult, the negligence of the
parents is no defense.*

> Gowan *v.* Brooklyn Cross-town R. R. Co., 2 Mo.
>   Bul. 12.
> McGarry *v.* Loomis, 63 N. Y. 104.
> Ihl *v.* Forty-second St. R. R. Co., 47 N. Y. 317.
> Birkett *v.* Knickerbocker Ice Co., 41 Hun, 404.
> Cumming *v.* Brooklyn City R. R. Co., 104 N. Y. 669.

(c) Just here may be conveniently noticed a line of
cases in New York in which the whole question of contributory negligence of infants is summarily disposed of
as follows :

"I know of but one rule on the subject, as the law is
held with us, and I think it applies to all persons without
exception and makes no discrimination on account of age.
It is that degree of care which a person of ordinary prudence would exercise in the situation supposed."

> Honegsberger *v.* Second Ave. R. R. Co., 2 Abb.
>   Dec. 378.
> Burke *v.* Broadway & Seventh Ave. R. R. Co.,
>   34 How. Pr. 239.
> Solomon *v.* Central Park, &c. R. R. Co., 1 Sweeny,
>   298.

This rule is probably not to be understood as assuming that all children, of no matter how tender age, can be
personally negligent; it proceeds rather upon the theory
that there can be no case in which some one may not be
charged with contributory negligence ; that whenever the
child does what would be negligent in an adult, and is not
of sufficient age to be responsible for his actions, it fol-

lows as matter of law, that the parents were negligent in permitting him to get into danger.

The onus is then cast on the parents in every case of judging correctly of the responsibility of the child; and this directly affects the child himself, since he is bound by the contributory negligence of the parents.

To state the rule in other words: All persons, infants included, are bound to one rigid rule of ordinary prudence. If the person transgressing this rule be an adult, or any person *sui juris*, he is directly bound by his contributory negligence and his recovery barred. If *non sui juris*, the direct responsibility is shifted upon the parent or protector; the acts of the infant become proof positive of the negligence of the parent, and the infant is bound by the negligence of the parent and his recovery still barred. This seems a harsh rule. It is said in 16 Central L. J. p. 429; also in 6 Abb. N. C. p. 104, to be no longer the rule in this State; and the present current of decision does not appear to sustain it.

(d) The more approved rule seems to be that stated in Ryder *v.* New York, 50 Super. 220, where a child, while playing on the sidewalk, fell into an excavation. The court say:

" Whether *sui juris* or not, if she by want of such care and attention, on her own part, as could have been fairly expected and due from one of her years and knowledge of the nature of the danger to be guarded against, had caused this injury, such negligence on her part would go far to defeat this action. If *sui juris*, it would be negligence imputable to herself (Wendell *v.* R. R., 91 N. Y. 426; Thur-

ber *v.* R. R., 60 Id. 333–4). If *sui juris*, and her parents
had been negligent in leaving her free to run at large on
the sidewalk, defective as it was, and so near a dangerous
excavation, then their negligence, concurring with her
negligence, would defeat the action (Reynolds *v.* R. R.,
58 N. Y. 248; Ihl *v.* R. R., 47 Id. 322)."

(e) Assuming such acts or omissions on the part of the
child as are mentioned in (b) above, two questions commonly arise :

(1) Was the child *sui juris;* or to what, if any, degree
of care must it be held ?

(2) If not *sui juris*, did the negligence of the parent
contribute to the injury?

(f) As to the first question, courts have sometimes held
as matter of law that a child of a certain age was or was
not responsible for his acts so as to be chargeable with
his own negligence.

Thus in Hartfield *v.* Roper, 21 Wend. 615, it was held
that : " At the tender age of two or three years, and even
more, the infant cannot personally exercise that degree of
discretion which becomes instinctive at an advanced age,
and for which the law must make him responsible through
them if the doctrine of mutual care between the parties
using the road is to be enforced at all in his case." And
the same was held in Prendergast *v.* N. Y. C. & H. R. R.
Co., 58 N. Y. 652.

While in Messenger *v.* Dennie, 137 Mass. 197, it was held
that in case of a boy of eight years old his own acts were
as matter of law fatal to his recovery.

The question of how far young persons in particular cases are to be held responsible for their acts which in an adult would prevent a recovery, is, however, usually left to the jury to determine.

The rule is variously stated ; the following examples will suffice :

" The rule in regard to the negligence of an adult, and that in regard to that of an infant of tender years is quite different. The adult must give that care and attention for his own protection that is ordinarily exercised by persons of discretion and intelligence . . . Of the infant of tender years less discretion is required, and the degree depends upon his age and knowledge. The caution required is according to the maturity and capacity of the child, and is to be determined in each case by the attendant circumstances."

Chicago, &c. R. R. Co. v. Murray, 71 Ill. 601.
Government St. R. R. Co. v. Hanlon, 53 Ala. 70.

" There is no fixed age at which children are bound to exercise the same diligence as adults. The question of intelligence is always for the jury."

Houston Ry. Co. v. Simpson, 60 Tex. 103.

" The degree of care required of an infant, the omission of which will constitute negligence on her part, is to be measured in each case by the maturity and capacity of the individual."

Thurber v. Harlem Br. &c. R. R. Co., 60 N. Y. 326.

" The degree of care required of an infant depends upon

temperament, characteristics and surroundings, and is a
question for the jury in each particular case."

> Davis *v.* New York, N. H. & H. R. R. Co., 9 W.
> Dig. 522.

Other cases upon this point are :

> Railroad Co. *r.* Stout, 17 Wall. 657.
> Fallon *v.* Central Park, &c. R. R. Co., 64 N. Y. 13.
> Byrne *v.* N. Y. C. & H. R. R. Co., 83 N. Y. 620.
> Dowling *v.* N. Y. C. & H. R. R. R. Co., 90 N. Y. 670.
> Barry *v.* N. Y. C. H. R. R. R. Co., 92 N. Y. 289.
> Jones *v.* Utica, &c. R. R. Co., 36 Hun, 115.
> Ryan *v.* N. Y. C. & H. R. R. R. Co., 37 Hun, 186.
> McGuire *v.* Spence, 91 N. Y. 303.
> Kunz *v.* Troy, 5 N. Y. St. R. 642.
> Thurber *v.* Harlem Br., &c. R. R. Co., 69 N. Y.
> 326.
> Mangam *v.* Brooklyn Ry. Co., 38 N. Y. 455.
> McGovern *v.* N. Y. C., &c. R. R. Co., 67 N. Y. 417.
> Mowrey *v.* Cent. City Ry., 66 Barb. 43 ; 51 N. Y.
> 666.
> Miller *v.* McCloskey, 1 Civ. Pro. 252.
> Finklestein *r.* N. Y. C., &c. R. R. Co., 41 Hun, 34.
> Collins *v.* So. Boston Ry. Co.,(Mass.) 34 A.L. J. 292.

(g) Under the rule laid down in the Honegsberger case,
if the infant were not responsible for his acts which in an
adult would be negligence, it would follow at once that
his parents or protectors were negligent. This, however,
is not the recognized rule. On the contrary, the courts
incline to leave this question to the jury to determine.

> Mangam *v.* Brooklyn R. R. Co., 38 N. Y. 455.
> Prendergast *v.* N. Y. C. & R. R. Co., 58 N. Y. 652.
> Chrystal *v.* Troy & B. R. R. Co., 22 W. Dig. 551.
> Kunz *r.* Troy, 5 N. Y. St. R. 642.

Thus it has been held not *per se* negligence to send

children of certain ages to school, or otherwise into possible danger, without protection.

Drew *v.* Sixth Ave. R. R. Co., 26 N. Y. 49.
McGovern *v.* N. Y. C., &c. R. R. Co., 67 N.Y. 417.
Ihl *v.* Forty-second St. R. R. Co., 47 N.Y. 317.
Stafford *v.* Rubens, (Ill.) 3 No. East. R. 568.

And yet it has been recently held as matter of law that the parents were so negligent that there could be no recovery.

Schindler *v.* N. Y., Lake E. & W. R. R. Co., 1 N.Y. St. Rep. 289.
Doran *v.* Troy, 22 W. Dig. 230.

(h) While a child of tender years is not held to the same degree of diligence as an adult, when a child complains of wrongs to himself, he cannot recover if he was the heedless instrument of his own injury.

Flood *v.* Buffalo, &c. R. R. Co., 23 W. Dig. 501.

It seems to have been usually held in this State, however, that the same rules would govern under like circumstances, whether the action were brought by the child itself or by the parent.

(i) In many States the doctrine of imputed negligence of a parent to bar recovery by a child does not seem to prevail, where the action is brought by the child.

Huff *v.* Ames, (Neb.) 30 Alb. L. J. 339.
Citing Daley *v.* Norwich, &c. R. R. Co., 26 Conn. 591.
Cleveland, &c. R. R. Co. *v.* Manson, 30 Ohio St. 451.
No. Pa. R. R. Co. *v.* Mahoney, 57 Penn. St. 187.
Whirley *v.* Whiteman, 1 Head, 610.
Government St. Ry. Co. *v.* Hanlon, 53 Ala. 70.
Norfolk, &c. R. R. Co. *v.* Ormsby, 27 Gratt. 455.

But may prevent recovery by the parent suing for services.

> Huff r. Ames, *supra*.
> Citing Glassey v. Hestonville, &c. Ry. Co., 57
>   Penn. St. 172.
> Louisville, &c. Canal Co. v. Murphy, 9 Bush 522.
> Oil City Bridge Co. r. Jackson, (Pa.) 36 Alb.
>   L. J. 36.

12. Imputed negligence. (a) *One who rides in the conveyance of another, of the management of which that other has the entire control, and the passenger has none, and is himself without negligence, is not bound by the other's negligence contributing to the injuries.*

> Chapman r. N. H. R. R. Co., 19 N. Y. 341.
> Colegrove v. N. Y. & N. H. R. Co., 20 N. Y. 492.
> Webster v. H. R. R. R. Co., 38 N. Y. 260.
> Metcalf r. Baker, 11 Abb. Pr. N. S.431.
> Platz v. Cohoes, 24 Hun, 101; 8 Abb. N. C. 392; 89
>   N. Y. 219.
> Dyer r. Erie Ry. Co., 71 N. Y. 228.
> Robinson v. N. Y. C., &c. R. R. Co., 66 N. Y. 11.
> Scott v. Wood, 18 W. Dig. 441.
> St. Clair St. Ry. Co. r. Eadie, (Ohio) 32 A. L. J. 64.
> Follman v. Mankato, (Minn.) 34 A. L. J. 391.
> Carlisle v. Brisbane, (Pa.) 34 A. L. J. 507.
> Gaylord v. Syracuse, &c. R. R. Co., 23 W. Dig.
>   396.
> Harvey r. New York, &c. R. R. Co., 23 W. Dig.
>   198.
> McCallum v. Long Island R. R. Co., 38 Hun, 569.
> Masterson v. New York C., &c. R. R. Co, 84 N. Y.
>   247.
> Callahan v. Sharp, 16 W. Dig. 505.
> But see Brown v. N. Y. C. R. R., 32 N. Y. 597.

In some of the above cases, the person injured was a passenger of a common carrier; in others, not; in some, was riding gratuitously; in others, for hire. But the same general rule was held to apply.

The above rule would seem to be at variance with the English case of Thorogood *v.* Bryan, 8 Common Bench, 115, in which it was held that a passenger in a coach was bound by the contributory negligence of the driver (see, however, remarks upon that case at 19 N. Y. 343, and 38 N. Y. 262).

(b) *Where, however, the vehicle was under the control of the person injured, or, if an infant non sui juris, of its parent or protector, the rule is otherwise.*

Doran *v.* Troy, 22 W. Dig. 230.

In such cases the vehicle may have been under the immediate control of the person injured or the protector, or else the driver may have been his agent or servant.

In Callahan *v.* Sharp, 16 W. Dig. 505, it was held that a person having a livery carriage and driver was not bound by the negligence of the driver (thus overruling S. C., 27 Hun, 85).

Of course, if the child were *sui juris* the negligence of the parent cannot be imputed to it.

Callahan *v.* Sharp, *supra.*
St. Clair St. Ry. Co. *v.* Eadie, (Ohio) 32 Alb. L. J.
64.

In the former case the child was sixteen years of age; in the latter, thirteen.

13. Imminent danger. *Where one is compelled to act at once in presence of immediate danger, it is not, as matter of law, contributory negligence that he did not exercise the best possible judgment.*

Bernhard v. R., &c. R. R. Co., 1 Abb. Dec. 131.
Buel v. N. Y. C. R. R. Co. 31 N. Y. 314.
Coulter v. Am , &c. Ex. Co., 56 N. Y. 585.
Twomley v. Cent. Pk., N. & E. R. R. R. Co., 69 N. Y. 158.
Lowery v. Manhattan Ry. Co., (N. Y.) 1 No. East. R. 608.
Dyer v. Erie Ry. Co., 71 N. Y. 228.
Voak v. No. C. Ry. Co., 75 N. Y. 320.
Cuyler v. Decker, 20 Hun, 173.
Steiverman v. White, 48 Super. 523.
Helmrich v. Hart, 16 W. Dig. 356.
Karr v. Parks, 40 Cal. 188.
Lawrence v. Green, (Cal.) 11 Pac. R. 750.
Stevenson v. Chicago, &c. R. R. Co., 18 Fed. Rep. 493.
Barton v. Springfield, 110 Mass. 131.
Siegrist v. Arnot, 10 Mo. Ap. 197.
Gunz v. Chicago, &c. Ry. Co., 25 A. L. J. 36.
Schultz v. Chicago, &c. Ry. Co., 44 Wis. 638.

Similar to the above—a person who, in a desperate alternative, is injured while attempting to save the lives of others, is not necessarily guilty of contributory negligence.

Roll v. N. C. Ry. Co., 15 Hun, 496. 80 N. Y. 647.
Eckert v. L. I. R. R. Co., 43 N. Y. 502.
Spooner v. D., L. & W. R. R. Co., 1 N. Y. St. Rep. 558.

14. Comparative negligence. In some States it is held that the negligence of plaintiff and defendant may be compared, and recovery had or refused, according to the preponderance of evidence.

Ivens v. Cincinnati, &c. Ry. Co., (Ind.) 2 No. East. R. 134.
Chicago, &c. Ry. Co. v. Payne, 59 Ill. 534.
Chicago, &c. Ry. Co. v. Dimick, 96 Id. 42.
Calumet Iron, &c. Co. v. Martin, (Ill.) 3 No. East. R. 456.
Dush v. Fitzhugh, 2 Lea (Tenn.) 307.
Hughes v. Muscatine, &c. Co., 44 Iowa, 672.

So far as this means merely that slight negligence on the part of the plaintiff may not be fatal as against gross neligence of the defendant, the New York courts have gone far to hold it, through rejecting the doctrine of comparative negligence as held in other States.

Clark v. Kirwan, 4 E. D. Smith, 21.
Green v. Erie Ry. Co., 11 Hun, 333.
McGrath v. H. R. R. R. Co., 32 Barb. 144.

In the Green case, the court hold that if the defendant by the use of ordinary care could have prevented the injury, the plaintiff may recover, though his negligence contributed to the injury.

So in case of a child.

Connery v. Slavin, 23 W. Dig. 545.

15. Acts held not negligent to bar recovery.

Playing in street.

McGuire v. Spence, 91 N. Y. 303.
Kunz v. Troy, 5 N. Y. St. R. 642.

Standing in street.

Hussey v. Ryan, (Md.) 4 East. R. 462.

Driving in dark night in country without lantern.

Chamberlin v. Ossipee, 60 N. H. 212.
Daniels v. Lebanon, 58 N. H. 294.

Deviating from street line to pass excavation.

Vale v. Bliss, 50 Barb. 358.

Driving in dark and allowing horses to pick their way.

Rector *v.* Pierce, 3 T. & C. 416.

16. **Aggravating injury by subsequent carelessness.** While this subject does not come strictly within that of negligence contributory to the injury, its practical bearing is analogous, and it will be considered here.

The rule may be stated as follows :

One who is injured by the negligence of another is bound to use ordinary care to effect his cure and restoration; but he is not responsible for a mistake, and when he acts in good faith and under the advice of a competent physician, even if it is erroneous, the error will not shield the wrong-doer.

Lyons *v.* Erie Ry. Co., 57 N. Y. 489.
Hope *v.* Troy & L. R. R. Co., 40 Hun, 438.
Loser *v.* Humphrey, 41 Ohio St. 378.
Pullman, &c. Co. *v.* Bluhm, 109 Ill. 20.

In Hope *v.* Troy & Lansingburgh R. R. Co., where there was evidence that the plaintiff had exposed herself after the injury, and her recovery was hindered thereby, the court say the question of her contributory negligence "depended on whether she went out against her own judgment, recklessly and carelessly, or whether she had occasion to go out, and felt she could do so without being guilty of want of fair care and caution."

(a) The evidence of such negligence is proper in mitigation of damages.

Carpenter *v.* Blake, 75 N. Y. 12.
Crete *v.* Childs, 11 Neb. 252.

CHAPTER XIV.

1. **Ice as an obstruction.** In northern latitudes, where snow falls and ice forms, a very large number of injuries are caused by falling upon the streets and sidewalks thus rendered slippery. These give rise to endless litigations, in which usually municipal corporations are defendants, although in some instances individuals are charged upon the theory that the ice was caused by their acts.

In these actions it is usually sought to charge municipal corporations upon the ground of the general liability to keep their streets in reasonably safe condition for travel. They are charged with faults of omission—not of commission.

The principles of law governing these cases are the same as in case of other obstructions rendering streets unsafe, and many of this class of cases are cited under the respective subjects which they illustrate.

It is only purposed to notice here some discussion as to when ice forms an obstruction at all so that a city may be charged with negligence in not removing it

[157]

(a) That ice and snow often render streets less safe than they otherwise would be, is self-evident. But much difference of opinion has arisen as to whether ice, though admittedly dangerous, is therefore such an obstruction as will charge a city with negligence.

There is probably no dispute but that snow and ice may exist upon a street in such shape as to form an obstruction; for instance, when it is heaped up, or presents a rough or uneven surface.

> Street v. Holyoke, 105 Mass. 82.
> McAuley v. Boston, 113 Mass. 503.
> Providence v. Clapp, 17 How. (U. S.) 161.
> McLaughlin v. Corry, 77 Penn. 109.

The distinction has often been taken that while ice in ridges or hummocks may be termed an obstruction, smooth ice is not.

> Stanton v. Springfield, 12 Allen, 566.
> Luther v. Worcester, 97 Mass. 268.
> Pinkham v. Topsfield, 104 Mass. 78.
> Broburg v. Des Moines, 63 Iowa, 523.
> Chicago v. McGiven, 78 Ill. 347.
> Smyth v. Bangor, 72 Maine, 249.
> Mauch Chunk v. Kline, 100 Penn. St. 119.

In Stanton v. Springfield, the court say : "No reported case is found, in which it has been decided that a way is defective merely because it is slippery, if in all other respects in good order and properly constructed, and the ice constituting no obstruction except by its smoothness."

Although this distinction has probably not been squarely taken in any decision in New York, yet stress is laid in many cases upon the fact that the ice in given cases was in fact uneven.

In Durkin v. Troy, 61 Barb. 437, and Mosey v. Troy, Id. 580, the respects of counsel were paid to the law of Massachusetts cases holding to the distinction, but the court seems in neither case to have found the determination of the question necessary.

In the following cases it has been recognized as a rule that glare and smooth ice upon a sidewalk may be as much an obstruction as that which is rough or uneven.

> Cloughessy v. Waterbury, 51 Conn. 405.
> Kinney v. Troy, 38 Hun, 285.

See also dissenting opinion in

> Muller v. Newburgh, 32 Hun, 24.

It is true that a rule which should make municipal corporations liable for every injury caused by their streets being rendered unsafe by the elements would be unjust. It is in view of this evident difficulty that it is often held that cities cannot be held accountable for obstructions caused by the storms of the season unless they have sufficient time, after notice, actual or constructive, to make the streets safe.

> Gibson v. Johnson, 4 Ill. Ap. 288.
> See also cases cited at page 124.

But that would seem the more reasonable rule which treats that as an obstruction which renders the street unsafe, no matter what its nature or how it may be caused, and one for which a city may be liable under proper circumstances, but leaves the jury to determine each particular case with reference to the elements of reasonable care and notice.

It is true that ice naturally becomes ridged and uneven by accumulation, and that accumulations of ice may be more exactly obstructions than ice which is smooth.

Moreover, that accumulation implies time, and time is an element of constructive notice. But it would seem that the reasoning is fallacious of those cases in which smooth ice is deemed to be not an obstruction for which a city may be liable; first, in that it fails to recognize the principle that safety is the thing to be achieved, and that whatever tends to produce unsafety is an obstruction within the use intended for the word in this connection; and second, in failing to recognize that smooth ice may have been just as long accumulating as rough, and constructive notice to the city may be just as well established.

(b) In some cases where cities have been held liable the defect has been caused in part by the ice and in part by the defective walk beneath.

> Atchison r. King, 9 Kan. 553.
> Mauch Chunk v. Kline, 100 Pa. St. 119.

In the latter case, the ice formed over cobble-stones laid between the flat stones upon the walk.

2. **Injuries by coasters.** Attempts have been made to charge municipal corporations with liability for injuries sustained by reason of coasting upon their streets.

Two classes of cases arise.

(a) Where recovery is sought upon the general ground

that coasting renders the streets unsafe, and so it is a defect which the city should remedy.

Upon this it was held that no such liability exists, in

Faulkner r. Aurora, 85 Ind. 130.
Shepherd r. Chelsea, 4 Allen, 113.
Pierce v. New Bedford 129 Mass. 534.
Hutchinson r. Concord, 41 Vt. 271.
Ray v. Manchester, 46 N. H. 59.
Lafayette r. Timberlake, 88 Ind. 330.
Calwell r. Boone, 51 Iowa, 687.

In Faulkner r. Aurora, it was also held that the city would neither be liable because of its failure to prohibit coasting by ordinance, nor for the failure of its officers to enforce an ordinance prohibiting coasting upon the streets.

(b) Where the city licenses coasting generally or sets aside particular streets for that purpose. In such cases it is sought to charge the corporation as having licensed a nuisance.

In Baltimore r. Marriott, 9 Md. 160, the city was held liable upon that ground; and in Schultz v. Milwaukee, 49 Wis. 254, is a dictum to the same effect.

The contrary was held in

Burford r. Grand Rapids, 18 No. West. Rep. 571;
29 Alb. L. J. 263.
Steele r. Boston, 128 Mass. 583.

1(

CHAPTER XV.

SHIFTING LIABILITY. RECOVERY OVER.

A.   SHIFTING LIABILITY.

1. By ordinance. *A municipal corporation cannot relieve itself from liability for negligence in the care of its streets by imposing the same duty upon the owners of adjoining lots.*

> Wallace *v* New York, 18 How. Pr. 169.
> Wilson *v.* New York, 1 Denio, 595.
> Cushen *v.* Auburn, 22 W. Dig. 387.
> Baltimore *v.* Marriott, 9 Md. 160.
> Hayes *v.* Cambridge, 138 Mass. 461.
> Taylor *v.* Yonkers, 26 W. Dig. 376.

Though it has been held that a city may excuse itself from liability by an ordinance requiring one licensed to

[182]

obstruct the streets for building purposes to place lights at the obstruction.

McKenna *v.* New York, 47 Super. 541.

Also that it is proper to prove the existence of an ordinance as some evidence to warrant the presumption by the city that it would be obeyed.

Reed *v.* New York, 31 Hun, 311.
Knupfle *v.* Knickerbocker Ice Co., 84 N. Y. 488.

In Illinois it is held that a city has not the constitutional power to compel owners or occupants of premises to keep the sidewalks and gutters clear of snow and ice, or sprinkled with ashes or sand in case it cannot be removed.

Chicago *v.* O'Brien, 111 Ill. 532.

This is believed to be the rule nowhere else.

Notes of Cases, 31 Alb. L. J. 362.

2. By charter. *A charter provision requiring lot-owners to keep their sidewalks in repair does not raise the presumption that the lot-owner has done his duty, so as to free the city (there being no proof of any requisition on the lot-owner).*

Niven *v.* Rochester, 76 N. Y. 619.
Cain *v.* Syracuse, 29 Hun, 105; 95 N. Y. 83:
Cushen *v.* Auburn, 22 W. Dig. 387.

Nor where the municipal authorities are authorized to compel owners or occupants to repair sidewalks or in default to do it themselves, does the service of notice to repair upon the owner free the city.

Russell *v.* Canastota, 98 N. Y. 496.

3. By contract. *A municipal corporation cannot escape responsibility for non-observance of its duty to keep its streets in repair, upon the plea that it has contracted with another party to repair them.*

Jacksonville *v.* Drew, 19 Flor. 106.

4. Obstruction by railroad. *A municipal corporation is liable when the obstruction is placed by a railroad company, the same as though it were placed by an individual.*

Sides *v.* Portsmouth, 59 N. H. 24.

And this is true whether the railroad company used the street under license from the city,

Campbell *v.* Stillwater, 32 Minn. 308.

or under a statute imposing a liability to keep the street in repair.

Tierney *v.* Troy, 41 Hun, 120.

B. Recovery Over.

1. General rule. *Where a person has negligently or unlawfully created an obstruction or defect in a street of a municipal corporation, and the latter has been compelled to pay a judgment recovered against it, for damages sustained by an individual caused by such defect, it has an action over against such person.*

Port Jervis *v.* First Nat. Bk. of P. J., 96 N. Y. 550.
Rochester *v.* Montgomery, 72 N. Y. 65.
Seneca Falls *v.* Zalinski, 8 Hun, 571.
Troy *v.* Troy & L. R. R. Co., 49 N. Y. 657.
Brooklyn *v.* Brooklyn City R. R. Co., 47 N. Y. 475.
Catterlin *v.* Frankfort, 79 Ind. 547.
Robbins *v.* Chicago, 4 Wall. 657.
Lowell *v.* Short, 4 Cush. 275.
Boston *v.* Worthington, 10 Gray, 496.

2. Grounds of liability. (a) *Licensee.* In case the obstruction was caused by a licensee, the right of recovery over depends upon his contract, express or implied, to perform the act permitted in such a manner as to protect the public from danger and the municipality from liability.

> Port Jervis *v.* First Nat. Bank, 96 N. Y. 550.
> Brooklyn *v.* Brooklyn City R. R. Co., 47 N. Y. 475.
> Congreve *v.* Morgan, 18 N. Y. 84.
> Troy *v.* Troy & L. R. R. Co., 49 N. Y. 657.

In the first two cases, the liability was implied; in the last, expressed in the contract.

And the fact that the obstruction was made with the knowledge of the city places the person at fault on the same ground as the licensee.

> Seneca Falls *v.* Zalinski, 8 Hun, 571.

In such a case the licensee can not defend upon the ground that the work was done for him by an independent contractor.

> Robbins *v.* Chicago, 4 Wall. 657.

(b) *Contractor.* In case of work done for the city upon contract, the liability of the contractor must be expressed, and in case it is not and a judgment is procured against the city it cannot recover over against the contractor.

> Buffalo *v.* Holloway, 7 N. Y. 493.

(c) *Wrong-doer.* A person causing a street to be unsafe while doing an act without contract or license is liable to recovery over, upon the principle that he is a guarantor of the safety of the street.

3. Abutting owner. *The abutting owner is not without statute or charter liable for the care of streets. In such a case there can be no recovery over.*

Fulton *v.* Tucker, 5 T. & C. 621.

4. Notice. Notice of suit brought and opportunity to defend is usually given the person causing the obstruction, by the corporation intending to hold him to recovery over.

The nature and precise effect of this notice give rise to some questions.

(a) Express notice is unnecessary. It is enough that the party knew the suit was pending and might have defended it.

Robbins *v.* Chicago, 4 Wall. 657.
Port Jervis *v.* First Nat. Bk., 96 N. Y. 550.
Barney *v.* Dewey, 13 Johns. 224.
Beers *v.* Pinney, 12 Wend. 309.
Heiser *v.* Hatch, 86 N. Y. 614.

(b) The omission to give notice does not go to the right of action, but simply changes the burden of proof, and imposes upon the party against whom the action was recovered the necessity of again litigating and establishing all the actionable facts.

Port Jervis *v.* First Nat. Bk., *supra.*
Aberdeen *v.* Blackmar, 6 Hill, 324.
Bridgeport Ins. Co. *v.* Wilson, 34 N. Y. 275.
Binsse *v.* Wood, 37 N. Y. 526.

(c) With notice, the record of the judgment against the city is competent evidence against the obstructor, and is conclusive as to his liability and as to the amount of recovery.

Troy v. T. & L. R. R. Co., 49 N. Y. 657.

Conclusive so far as relates to the cause of action, amount of damages, and other matters necessarily involved therein.

Seneca Falls v. Zalinski, 8 Hun, 571.

Conclusive both as to liability of corporation to person injured and as to any matter which might have been urged as a defense; so as to contributory negligence.

Rochester v. Montgomery, 72 N. Y. 65.
Boston v. Worthington, 10 Gray, 496.

As to the measure of damages, some question of its conclusiveness in cases where the liability depends on contract was raised in Brooklyn <i>v.</i> Brooklyn City R. R. Co., 47 N. Y. at p. 481, but it is assumed to apply to such a case in Rochester <i>v.</i> Montgomery, at p. 67.

PART II.

PRACTICE.

THE grouping of the following subjects under the generic head of practice, will undoubtedly form an arbitrary arrangement and one not strictly correct in many particulars. The idea is, however, to take the position, as well as may be, of the practitioner to whom a city-negligence case is brought, and to consider some of the practical questions that are likely to arise prior to and during the trial.

CHAPTER I.

STATUTE OF LIMITATIONS.

1. Introductory.
2. Action by person injured.
3. Action for loss of services.
4. Injuries resulting in death.
5. Statute retroactive.
6. 62 How. Pr. 255.
7. Cohoes charter.
8. Schenectady charter.
9. In Oswego.
10. Limitation of notice.

[168]

1. Introductory. The very first question to consider is whether or not the time has elapsed within which an action may be brought. That answered in the affirmative, all further labor is wasted.

The statutes of different States being different, no attempt will be made to consider them outside the State of New York, nor will all the special statutes relating to the several municipalities within the State be separately treated.

It will be found that under different circumstances three distinct rules apply: First, when the action is brought by the person injured; second, by a husband or parent for loss of services; third, for injuries resulting in death.

2. Action by person injured. *An action by the person injured, to recover damages for a personal injury, resulting from negligence, must be commenced within three years from the date of the injury.*

> Code Civ. Pro. § 383, subd. 5.
> Dickinson v. New York, 92 N. Y. 584.
> Watson v. Forty-second St. R. R. Co., 93 N. Y. 522.
> Webber v. Herkimer, &c. R. R. Co., 35 Hun, 44.

Prior to 1876, the old Code provided that "an action . . . for any other injury to the person . . . of another, not arising on contract, and not hereinafter enumerated" should come within the six years limitation class.

By Laws 1876, ch. 431, section 7, an action for injury to the person was put in the one year class.

But upon the enactment of the new Code in 1877 the limitation was extended to six years, with a special exception in the case of personal injuries resulting from negligence, which were put in the three years class, as above stated.

In cities of 50,000 inhabitants and over, the action must be commenced within one year.   Laws of 1886, p. 501, § 1.

3. Action for loss of services. *In this case the action is brought by a husband to recover for loss of the services of his wife by reason of an injury to her person, the six years limitation applies.*

Groth *v.* Washburn, 34 Hun, 509.

This upon the ground that an action is brought, not for a personal injury at all, but for the result of an injury to " his rights, interests and property."

4. Injuries causing death. *In case the action is brought by an executor or administrator of a person whose injuries resulted in death, it must be brought within two years.*

Code Civ. Pro. § 1902.

The preceding statute to the same effect was contained in ch. 450, Laws 1847, as amended, Laws 1849, ch. 256, and Laws 1870, ch. 78.

Under these statutes has been decided :

Bonnell *v.* Jewett, 24 Hun, 524.

5. Statute retroactive. *Where one period of limitation is in effect at the time of the injury, and another at the commencement of the action, the latter prevails.*

Dubois r. Kingston, 20 Hun, 500.
Reversed on other grounds, 102 N. Y. 219.
Watson r. Forty-second St. R. R. Co., 93 N. Y. 522.
Hirsch r. Buffalo, 21 W. Dig. 312.

The contrary was held in :

Carpenter r. Shimer, 24 Hun, 464.
Goillotel r. New York, 87 N. Y. 440.

(Observe that in both the above Court of Appeals decisions the ruling favors the plaintiff.)

6. Theory of 62 How. Pr. 255. It was held by the special term, in Dickinson v. New York, upon a demurrer to the defense of the statute of limitations, that an action brought against the city for failure to keep its streets in repair, was for a wrongful act rather than for negligence ; and hence that the six years limitation applied. This was reversed by the general term (28 Hun, 254), and the latter judgment affirmed, at 92 N. Y. 584.

7. Under Cohoes charter. The provision of the Cohoes charter (Laws 1869, ch. 912, title 13, section 5), that no action against the city on a contract obligation or liability, express or implied, shall be commenced except within one year after the cause of action has accrued, was held to apply to actions upon contracts only, in

McGaffin r. Cohoes, 74 N. Y. 387.

8. Schenectady charter. Laws 1882, ch. 294, provides that all actions for defective streets must be brought within one year.

Held constitutional in

> Van Vranken *v*. Schenectady, 31 Hun, 516.

9. In Oswego. The period is fixed by statute at one year.

> Laws 1877, ch. 127, § 15.
> Dalrymple *v*. Oswego, 25 W. Dig. 332.

10. Limitation of notice. It should be added here that the time for presentation of notice of claim is also sometimes limited. Thus, in each of the following cities to three months.

Albany:

> Laws 1883, p. 364, § 45.

Schenectady :

> 1 Laws 1882, p. 359, § 4.

Oswego:

> 1 Laws 1877, p. 132, § 15.

CHAPTER II.

NOTICE OF CLAIM.

HAVING decided in a given case that it is not too late to seek a remedy, the next requisite is a presentation of a claim for relief, where required, to some officer or department of the corporation designated by statute for that purpose. The several statutes will not be considered. Sometimes they relate to entire States, sometimes to single cities.

[173]

In New York there are a general law, making the recovery of costs in certain actions against municipal corporations dependent on the presentation of a claim, and numerous special charter provisions, the nature and effect of the two being quite distinct. And, in addition to these, a general provision for notice to the corporation attorney in cities of 50,000 population or over.

A. New York Statute as to Costs.

1. Code Civ. Pro. § 3245. "Costs cannot be awarded to the plaintiff in an action against a municipal corporation in which the complaint demands a judgment for a sum of money only, unless the claim upon which the action is founded was, before the commencement of the action, presented for payment to the chief fiscal officer of the corporation."

2. Act of 1859. This is the successor of a similar act (Laws 1859, ch. 262, § 2), differing from it only in restricting the demand to one for a sum of money only.

3. Adjudications have been had upon various points relative to this section: such as that it does not apply in justices' courts.

Marsh v. Lansingburgh, 31 Hun, 514.

That it does not apply to costs on appeal.

Utica Water Works v. Utica, 31 Hun, 426.

That in Kingston the treasurer is the chief fiscal officer.

Dressel v. Kingston, 32 Hun, 526.

That in Buffalo presentation to the common council is sufficient,

Williams r. Buffalo, 25 Hun, 301.

and was in Rochester until 1880,

Butler r. Rochester, 4 Hun, 321.

when the treasurer was by statute made chief fiscal officer.

Baine r. Rochester, 85 N. Y. 523.

That the lack of power in the fiscal officer to adjust and pay the claim, does not excuse failure to present it.

Baine r. Rochester, *supra*.
Judson v. Olean, 40 Hun, 158.

Contra,

Childs r. West Troy, 23 Hun, 68.

That in Hornellsville the chief fiscal officer is the board of trustees, and not the treasurer.

Gage r. Hornellsville, 41 Hun, 87.

That plaintiff's failure to get costs does not give costs to defendant.

Baine v. Rochester, *supra*.

4. **No application in actions for wrongs.** But all these, and other adjudications upon this statute, are rendered useless here in light of the recent decision of the court of appeals, that the statute applies only to actions upon contract.

A glance at some decisions upon this subject may be interesting.

In Hart *v.* Brooklyn, 36 Barb. 226, decided in 1862, the act of 1859 was held to apply to negligence cases.

In McClure *v.* Supervisors of Niagara, 3 Abb. Dec. 83 (1867), it was held to not so apply ; and the court rely upon the reasoning of Howell *v.* Buffalo, 15 N. Y. 512 (which, however, arose under a special provision of the Buffalo charter), and assumes that if the court in deciding the McClure case had had its attention called to the Hart case, its decision would have been conformed to it.

In Childs *v.* West Troy, 23 Hun, 68 (1880), it was also held to not apply, but the decision was placed strictly upon the ground of the inability of the municipal officers to audit a claim for a tort.

In Dressel *v.* Kingston, 32 Hun, 526 (1884), it was decided by a divided court, upon the supposed authority of Baine *v.* Rochester, 85 N. Y. 523, that the claim in a negligence case must be presented, in order to obtain costs.

This was cited in Judson *v.* Olean, 40 Hun, 158, but was unnecessary to the determination of the case.

The same was assumed in Fisher *v.* Cortland, 25 W. Dig. 253.

In Taylor *v.* Cohoes, 35 Alb. L. J. 357, the court of appeals have held directly that § 3245 and the act of 1859 apply only to actions upon contract, and point out in the opinion that the Baine case decided nothing to the contrary.

B. New York Act of 1886.

1. Statute. It is provided by chapter 572 of the Laws of 1886, page 501, section 1, as follows:

" No action against the mayor, aldermen and commonalty of any city in this State, having fifty thousand inhabitants, or over, for damages for personal injuries alleged to have been sustained by reason of the negligence of such mayor, aldermen and commonalty, or of any department, board, officer, agent, or employee of said corporation, shall be maintained, unless the same shall be commenced within one year after the cause of action therefor shall have accrued, nor unless notice of the intention to commence such an action, and of the time and place at which the injuries were received, shall have been filed with the counsel to the corporation, or such other proper law officer thereof, within six months after such cause of action shall have accrued."

2. Application. This section in respect to the presentation of claims to the corporation attorney, or counsel, is in addition to the notice required to be served upon the comptroller of the city, or other officer, by charter, considered below ; and the notice here provided for should probably not be served until the expiration of the term of notice provided in such charters.

C. Under Charters.

1. Introductory. The charters of many municipal corporations provide especially for the presentation of a

12

statement of the claim, sometimes as a condition precedent to recovery at all ;

> Charter of New York, 2 Laws 1882, p. 305, § 1104.
> Charter of Albany, Laws 1883, p. 364, § 45.
> Charter of Troy, 1 Laws 1872, p. 336, § 10.
> Charter of Buffalo, 2 Laws 1870, p. 1179, § 7.

sometimes as affecting only the question of costs.

> Charter of Utica, Laws 1862, p. 76, § 123.
> Charter of Binghamton, 1 Laws 1867, p. 642, § 7.
> Charter of Auburn, Laws 1879, p. 99, § 140.

In the former case, the statute sometimes covers all
claims.

> Charter of New York, *supra.*

Sometimes all unliquidated claims.

> Charter of Buffalo, *supra.*

Sometimes all claims for injury to person or property.

> Charter of Troy, *supra.*

Sometimes claims arising from defective streets are
specified.

> Charter of Albany, *supra.*
> Charter of Oswego, Laws 1877, p. 132, § 15.
> Charter of Schenectady, 1 Laws 1882, p. 359, § 4.

Sometimes the statement must be verified.

> Charters of Albany and Troy.

2. **Application.** Under different charters, these provisions have been held to apply to negligence cases, in

> Nagel *v.* Buffalo, 34 Hun, 1.
> Duryea *v.* New York, 26 Hun, 120.

and that they do not, in

Quinlan r. Utica, 74 N. Y. 603.
Pomfrey r. Saratoga Springs, 104 N. Y. 459.

3. Construed prospectively. Such statutes are to be construed prospectively, and do not apply to cases where the injury was sustained before the law went into effect.

Williams v. Oswego, 25 Hun, 36.

4. Buffalo charter. Under the provision of the Buffalo charter, that all claims growing out of the water department should be presented to the water-board, held that this did not include claims for injuries caused by excavations in streets made by the water department.

Brusso v. Buffalo, 90 N. Y. 679.

D. General Provisions.

1. Introductory. Irrespective of the particular statutes requiring the presentation of claims, various questions arise as to which adjudications are of more than local value.

2. To whom presented. Must the claim be presented to the officer named, in person?

The answer to this question must of course depend largely upon the words of the statute.

In McCabe v. Cambridge, 134 Mass. 484, where the notice was required to be served on the city clerk, it was held sufficient to serve it, in his absence, upon his assistant in the city clerk's office.

In New York it has been held that under a charter providing for presentation to the Common Council, delivery to its clerk was sufficient.

Murphy v. Buffalo, 22 W. Dig. 284.

3. What to present. The Troy charter provides that " no civil action shall be maintained against the city by any person for injuries to person or property, unless it appear that the claim for which the action was brought was presented to the comptroller, with an abstract of the facts out of which the cause of action arose, duly verified by the claimant, and that said comptroller did not, within sixty days thereafter, audit the same."

Laws 1872, p. 336, § 10.

Under this it has recently been held at circuit, in one case, that the original claim must be presented, and not a copy ; in another case, the paper left with the comptroller was a copy, but the plaintiff's attorney testified that he presented the original to the comptroller at the same time at which he left the copy with him ; and the court declined to hold the service void.   The latter case, Magee v. Troy, is now on its way to the general term.

4. Amount claimed. It is sometimes important to know whether or not the amount claimed in the notice regulates the amount for which suit may be brought.

Under the Kansas statute, similar to N. Y. Code, § 3245, it has been held that the plaintiff is not deprived of his costs because he demanded more in the complaint than was claimed in the notice.

Wyandotte v. White, 13 Kan. 191.

And to the same effect it has been held in two New York cases, under charters making the presentation of a claim a pre-requisite to recovery.

> Minick v. Troy, 83 N. Y. 514.
> Reed v. New York, 97 N. Y. 620.

5. Contents of notice. What constitutes sufficient notice under a given statute is a question for the court.

> Chapman v. Nobleboro, 76 Maine, 427.

The object and general character of the notice have been well defined as "such precise information as would enable the officers to inquire into the facts intelligently."

> Shaw v. Waterbury, 46 Conn. 263.

The following decisions upon this point may be useful.

(a) *Place of injury.* Only a reasonable degree of particularity is required ;

> Tuttle v. Winchester, 50 Conn. 496.

sufficient if place designated with such certainty that it can be ascertained by the authorities,

> Fopper v. Wheatland, 59 Wis. 623.
> Fassett v. Roxbury, 56 Vt. 552.

even if in some particular the location be wrong,—

> McCabe v. Cambridge, 134 Mass. 484.

e. g., on the wrong side of the street.

> Cloughessy v. Waterbury, 51 Conn. 405.

It may be sufficient :

When it describes the place as at the corner of two ways, without specifying which corner.

> Sargent *v.* Lynn, 138 Mass. 599.

If it name the house, street, and side of street.

> Savory *v.* Haverhill, 132 Mass., 324.

If it describe an obstruction between two given residences, even though at some distance apart, and others were between them, if there is only one such obstruction in that locality.

> Melendy *v.* Bradford, 56 Vt. 148.

If it describe a large hole in a planking, though two smaller ones near.

> Lyman *v.* Hampshire Co., 138 Mass. 74.

But was held not sufficient when it described the *locus in quo* as

A "rough, hobbly and slippery" sidewalk between two named streets, which were 200 feet apart.

> Cronin *v.* Boston, 135 Mass. 110.

On north side of street, when accident really happened on south side.

> Shallow *v.* Salem, 136 Mass. 136.

On a given street which proved to be two miles long.

> Donnelly *v.* Fall River, 130 Mass. 115.

(b) *Time.* Held sufficient:

Naming day, unless time of day important.

Donnelly *v.* Fall River, 132 Mass. 294.
Savory *v.* Haverhill, Id. 324.

"Christmas morning."

Taylor *v.* Worcester, 130 Mass. 494.

Day held not sufficient.

White *v.* Stowe, 54 Vt. 510.

(c) *Cause.* It has been held sufficient to state that the fall was "consequent upon the icy and slippery condition of the said sidewalk."

Dalton *v.* Salem, 136 Mass. 278.

That the claimant was "thrown into a ditch."

Bailey *v.* Everett, 132 Mass. 441.

But not enough to state the cause simply as the "defective and dangerous condition of the way," or an obstruction in the way, without specifying the particular danger.

Nourse *v.* Victory, 51 Vt. 275.
Noonan *v.* Lawrence, 130 Mass. 161.
Roberts *v.* Douglass, (Mass.) 2 East. R. 114.

It has been held that a notice of injury by an iron grating will not cover a fall on ice.

McDougal *v.* Boston, 134 Mass. 149.

But the court declined to rule as matter of law that a notice of injury caused by "the improper grading of the said road and the want of proper railing by the side of said road," did not embrace an improper declivity of a gutter at the road side.

Spooner v. Freetown, 139 Mass. 235.

It is enough if it states the proximate cause.

Grogan v. Worcester, (Mass.) 2 East. R. 735.

(d) *Nature of injury.* It has been held that a notice stating that the claimant was "violently shaken up and jarred in his fall to the ground," permits proof of all the injuries sustained.

Wadleigh v. Mt. Vernon, 75 Me. 79.

That "injury to spine near shoulders" covers injury to spine between the shoulder blades.

Fassett v. Roxbury, 55 Vt. 552.

But that simply mentioning "injuries that I sustained" is not enough.

Low v. Windham, 75 Me. 113.

CHAPTER III.

A. The Complaint.

1. Code requisites. The New York Code prescribes the general requisites of a complaint as :

(1) Title of cause, and if in supreme court, name of county.

(2) Names of parties.

(3) "A plain and concise statement of the facts constituting each cause of action, without unnecessary repetition."

(4) Demand of judgment.

It is with a view to this system of pleading only that the following suggestions are given as to the preparation of a complaint against a municipal corporation for negligence-injuries.

[185]

2. Particular requisites. What are the " facts constituting a cause of action "?

It is believed that the following list embraces all the
usual requisites, and possibly also some which are unnecessary. It is believed to outline a safe pleading.

(a) State character of defendant ; that it is a domestic
municipal corporation.

(b) Its duty, statutory or otherwise, to keep its streets
reasonably safe for travel.

(c) That the place of injury was a street of the city.

(d) The location.

(e) The defect or obstruction.

(f) Notice thereof to the defendant.

(g) The negligence of the defendant.

(h) The care of the plaintiff.

(i) The injury.

(j) The damage.

(k) The presentation of notice under charter, with failure to audit, and expiration of time.

(l) Notice to law-officer under act of 1886.

In case the action is brought by a personal representative, add also :

(m) The fact of death.

(n) The authority of plaintiff to sue.

(o) The survival of beneficiaries.

If brought for loss of services of wife or child, add proper allegations for such purposes.

If brought for an infant by its guardian *ad litem*, allege appointment and qualification.

3. Adjudications. With regard to some of the above, certain decisions may be noted.

(a) The complaint must allege *negligence* of the defendant.

Rushville *v.* Poe, 85 Ind. 83.

(b) Also *notice* of defect, actual or constructive.

Noble *v.* Richmond, 31 Gratt. (Va.) 271.

Demurrable if not alleged.

Spiceland *v.* Alier, 96 Ind. 467.

(c) It is usually held that the *absence of contributory negligence* need not be pleaded.

Wolfe *v.* Supervisors of Richmond Co., 19 How.
Pr. 370.
Urquhart *v.* Ogdensburgh, 23 Hun, 75.
Lee *v.* Troy City Gas-Light Co., 98 N. Y. 115.
Street R.R. Co. *v.* Nolthenius, 40 Ohio St. 376.
Lopez *v.* Cent. Ariz. Mfg. Co., 1 Ariz. 484.
Holt *v.* Whatley, 51 Ala. 569.
Texas, &c. R. R. Co. *v.* Murphy, 47 Tex. 356.
Bedford, &c. R. R. Co. *v.* Rainbolt, 99 Ind. 561.

(d) As to the *nature of the injury* it is competent to prove permanent disease of the spine under an allegation of "great bodily injury."

Ehrgott *v.* New York, 96 N. Y. 264.

(e) *Damages.* All damages which are the direct result of the injury may be recovered under a general averment.

Cabot *v.* Kane, 1 N. Y. St. R. 495.

If a father would prove special damage until the majority of his infant son he must allege it.

Gilligan *v.* N. Y. & H. R. R. Co., 1 E. D. S. 453.

Complaint alleging general inability to pursue lawful business admits proof of nature of business and wages, and damages from interruption.

Luck *v.* Ripon, 52 Wis. 196.
Bloomington *v.* Chamberlain, 104 Ill. 268.

(f) *Place of injury.* Allegation of excavation " in and on " an alley, sustained by proof that it was adjacent to the alley.

Niblett *v.* Nashville, 12 Heisk. (Tenn.) 684.

(g) *Presenting claim.* When a statute makes notice pre-requisite to action against a city, it must be pleaded.

Wentworth *v.* Summit, 60 Wis. 281.
Dorsey *v.* Racine, Id. 292.
Reining *v.* Buffalo, 102 N. Y. 308.

Overruling

Nagel *v.* Buffalo, 34 Hun, 1.

The charter of New York city provides that " no action . . . shall be prosecuted or maintained, unless it shall appear by and as an allegation . . . in the complaint, . . . that at least thirty days have elapsed since the

claim . . . upon which said action . . . is founded
were presented to the comptroller, &c."

2 Laws 1883, p. 305, § 1104.

That of Troy provides that "no civil action shall be
maintained, unless it appears that the claim was presented," &c. (1 Laws 1872, p. 336, § 10), and the proof to
make it appear, of course, requires an allegation in the
pleading.

B. THE ANSWER.

The legal advisers of municipal corporations usually
employ stereotyped forms of answer, in which nearly
every allegation of the complaint is put in issue and contributory negligence set up as an affirmative defense.

Examples of these answers will be found, with other
forms, in an Appendix.

CHAPTER IV.

SELECTION OF JURORS.

1. Introductory. An interesting question has arisen in respect to the competency of the residents of a municipal corporation to sit as jurors in an action in which the city or village is interested.

On the one hand, it is evident that such persons are interested, for their eligibility to do jury duty at all depends upon a property qualification ; and a judgment against a municipal corporation is a charge in some degree upon every property owner within it.

On the other hand, in New York, where city and county are co-extensive, no jury could be empanelled under existing laws, for the trial of such an action.

2. Incompetent at common law. In Diveny *v.* Elmira, 51 N. Y. 506, the question presented was the direct one : "Is a resident and tax-payer of the defendant corporation incompetent as a juror?" And it was held that, in ab-

[190

sence of a statute to the contrary, they were incompetent. The court say : "The object of the law is to procure impartial, unbiased persons for jurors. *Omni exceptione majores.* They must have no interest in the subject matter of the litigation. In this case a verdict against the city would impose additional burdens upon all tax-paying residents thereof. Hence such residents are, at common law, incompetent to serve as jurors in a case in which the city is a party, or in which the city is directly interested."

3. Statutes. As to some municipalities it is specially provided by statute that residents and tax-payers shall not for that reason be incompetent as jurors in city cases.

The Troy statute is an example.

Laws 1816, ch. 1, § 16.

4. Rejection of competent juror. *The rejection of a competent juror is a ground of error, although the jurors who actually try the case are competent.*

Hildreth *v.* Troy, 101 N. Y. 234.

Upon the trial of this cause twelve persons drawn as jurors were rejected upon the ground that as residents of the city they were interested in the result of the action; the court and plaintiff's counsel not probably recalling the statute above cited. This was held error by both the higher courts.

The cases relied upon by plaintiff were :

Tweed *v.* Davis, 1 Hun, 252.
People *v.* Jewett, 3 Wend. 314.
Mullen *v.* Decker, 19 W. Dig. 426.
Grand Rapids, &c. Co. *v.* Jarvis, 30 Mich. 308.

The language relied on in Tweed *v.* Davis was that of
Mr. Justice Westbrook only, contained in his separate
opinion. Two jurors had been rejected on the ground of
incompetency, and their incompetency was conceded by
all the court. But Mr. Justice Westbrook adds : "So long
as the defendant was tried by twelve others who were
competent, we do not see that the rejection of these two,
conceding their competency, could in any way prejudice
him [the appellant]."

The case of People *v.* Jewett was not less celebrated
in its day than the Tweed case, it being the trial of the
alleged murderer of the Freemason, William Morgan.

In that case, in selecting the grand jury, all Free-
masons were excluded, and the court held that a challenge
to the array would not be allowed upon that ground, if
the jurors returned were unexceptionable and possessed
the statutory qualifications.

CHAPTER V.

THE PLAINTIFF'S CASE.

1. Introductory.
2. Incorporation.
3. Duty as to streets.
4. Presentation of notices.
5. Locus in quo.
6. The defect or obstruction.
7. The injury.
8. Burden of proof of negligence.
9. Notice.
10. Contributory negligence.
11. Damages.

The three subjects last named will be considered in separate chapters.

1. Introductory. *The burden is, speaking generally, upon the plaintiff to establish all the allegations of the complaint, so far as they are not admitted by the answer.*

It is purposed to consider briefly each of these requisites.

2. Incorporation. The incorporation of the city is usually admitted by the answer. If not, it need not be proven, unless it be denied by a verified answer.

Code Civ. Pro. § 1776.

The introduction of the charter is sufficient proof.

13   [193]

3. Duty as to streets. This, being statutory, may be proven by introducing the charter or act under which the city or village was incorporated, and especially those parts in which that subject is particularly provided for,—whether it be a direct provision or one making the common council commissioners of highways.

Ellis v. Lowville, 7 Lans. 434.

This duty is not increased by the passage of an ordinance requiring owners to remove snow and ice from in front of their property.

Stanton v. Springfield, 12 Allen, 566.

Nor by the neglect to enforce such ordinances.

Stillwell v. New York, 49 N. Y. Super. (17 J. & S.) 360.

4. Presentation of claim and of notice to law-officer. The service of notices, wherever required either by charter or general statute, might well be and often is admitted, since the original paper is in the possession of city officers.

Where, however, it is not admitted, its production may be compelled by notice to produce, or by subpœna *duces tecum*, or in failure thereof, proof may be made by producing a copy with oral evidence of the original.

5. The locus in quo, and that it was a street. That the locality of the accident was on a street, so as to charge

the municipality with its care, may, if disputed, be one of the most difficult questions in the case.

Where the street was designated as such in the charter, or was established by statutory proceeding, or declared such by statutory prescription, the matter of proof is of course easy. In the first case, it is necessary only to produce the charter ; in the second, to prove the proceeding under the statute ; in the third, to show user for the requisite time. The proof of user is not always wholly without difficulty, but it is in theory simple.

In case it is sought to prove the existence of a street by dedication, the proof is more complex. Here the intent to dedicate by the owner of the fee must be shown, and, independently of that, the acceptance by the public.

Part I., chap. IV. B, contains suggestions that may be useful in this connection.

In addition to what is there said, it may be added that where, by reason of the newness of streets, or otherwise, the question of acceptance by the city is in doubt, it is sometimes possible to show that a given map, containing the street, has been made or accepted by the city.

If the acceptance of the map be actual, it may be shown by the record of the proceedings of the common council : but it may be inferred from actions, as by the city using or distributing copies of the map.

So again, implied acceptance may sometimes be shown by proving that work had been done or ordered by the city upon the street,—such as the maintaining street lamps, hydrants, &c. Here again the minutes of the common council may come in play.

To obtain the minutes, if they are printed under the certificate of the clerk that such printing was done by direction of the common council, such printed volumes may be put in evidence. Otherwise, the city clerk may be subpœnaed to produce the original record.

If there is any evidence that the place was a public street, the plaintiff is entitled to go to the jury upon that question

Tierney *v.* Troy, 41 Hun, 120.

It should also be remembered that a way may be treated as a street by a city, and so become such so far as to charge the city with liability, though otherwise not a street.

See Part I., chap. V., B, 3.

6. The defect or obstruction. The existence of the condition which is claimed to be dangerous, and which caused the plaintiff's injury, must, of course, be proven by persons who knew of it.

Where one person testifies that he pointed to another the place where the accident occurred, it is competent for the other to testify as to the condition of the street before and at the time of the accident, although he was not then present.

Hirsch *v.* Buffalo, 21 W. Dig. 312.

Whether or not a given object constitutes an obstruction, or a street is defective, is a question ordinarily for the jury to determine.

For the purpose of proving the existence of the defect, it is competent :

To show the condition of the street the day after the injury.

De Forest r. Utica, 69 N. Y. 614.
Albilene r. Hendricks, (Kan.) 13 Pac. R. 121.

That it was in the same condition a few days before and after the accident.

Chicago r. Dalle, 115 Ill. 386.

That it was in the same condition ten days after, there being no evidence of change.

Berrenberg r. Boston, 137 Mass. 231.

But that the city authorities have improved the condition of a sidewalk since the injury to the plaintiff, is not an admission that it was previously defective.

Cramer v. Burlington, 45 Iowa, 627.

Nor, in New York, is it competent evidence.

Dougan r. Champlain Trans. Co., 56 N. Y. 1.
Payne r. T. & B. R. R. Co., 9 Hun, 526.
Morrell r. Peck, 24 Hun, 38.
Moore r. Birdsall, 22 W. Dig. 530.

Contra in Kansas.

Emporia r. Schmidling, 33 Kan. 485.

It is incompetent to prove that other sidewalks in the neighborhood were generally out of repair.

Ruggles v. Nevada, 63 Iowa, 185.

But if a sidewalk is unsafe for a long distance continuously, it may all be shown, though the accident was at one end.

> Armstrong r. Ackley, (Iowa) 32 No. W. R. 180.

7. **The injury.** This must be proven, as to the accident itself, by the plaintiff or others who were present; as to the extent of the injury, by the plaintiff and others who attended him, including physicians. The evidence bearing upon this point will be considered in connection with the subject of damages.

There must be positive proof that the injury was the direct result of tho defect.

> Monohan v. Cohoes, 8 W. Dig. 528.

The plaintiff has the right to prove the *res gestœ*.

> Hallahan v. N. Y., L. E. & W. Ry Co., 102 N. Y. 194.

But declarations of the injured person after his injury and while being taken away, as to how it happened (the injury resulting in his death), are not competent.

> Martin v. N. Y., &c. R. R. Co., 25 W. Dig. 197.

8. **Burden of proof of negligence.** *The burden of proving the negligence of the defendant is on the plaintiff.*

> Cordell r. New York Central, &c. R. R. Co., 75 N. Y. 330.
> Hale v. Smith, 78 N. Y. 480.
> Frech r. Phila., &c. R. R. Co., 39 Md. 574.
> Wardwell r. New York, 1 N. Y. St. R. 784.
> Merrill r. North Yarmouth, (Me.) 4 E. R. 936.

It will not be inferred from the mere fact of the accident.

> Baltimore El. Co. v. Neal, (Md.) 5 Atl. R. 338.

The plaintiff is not, however, bound to prove negligence beyond a reasonable doubt.

Seybolt *r.* N. Y., L. E. &c. R. R. Co., 95 N. Y. 562.
Wiedmer *r.* N. Y. El. R. Co., 41 Hun, 284.

It may be proved by circumstances.

Hart *r.* Hudson R. Br. Co., 80 N. Y. 622.

For the purpose of establishing negligence, the absence of gas or light may be considered.

Indianapolis *r.* Scott, 72 Ind. 196.
O'Hagan *v,* Dillon, 76 N. Y. 170.

CHAPTER VI.

NOTICE.

A. ACTUAL NOTICE.

1. Evidence held competent. For the purpose of charging a city with actual notice of an obstruction or defect, the following evidence has been held competent:

(a) That a councilman had notice of it.

> Logansport v. Justice, 74 Ind. 378.

(b) Or a highway surveyor of a New England town.

> Rogers v. Shirley, 74 Me. 144.

(c) That the street commissioners knew the whole

[200]

sidewalk was old, rotten and unsafe, though ignorant of the looseness of the particular plank causing the injury.

Ripon v. Bettel, 30 Wis. 614.

(d) That a street commissioner was informed of the defect—coupled with the presumption that he performed his duty of inquiring, after such information.

Welch v. Portland, 77 Me. 384.

(e) A book kept at the office of the city messenger, containing complaint of the condition of the street.

Blake v. Lowell, (Mass.) 9 No. East. R. 627.

(f) The report of a street commissioner that a street was unsafe.

Bond v. Biddeford, 75 Me. 538.

(g) Resolution of city council directing repairs of a sidewalk.

Erd v. St. Paul, 22 Minn. 443.
Aurora v. Pennington, 92 Ill. 564.

2. Evidence not competent. On the other hand, proof of repair after the accident is not competent to prove notice.

Morse v. Minn. & St. L. R. R. Co., (Minn.) 28 A. L. J. 320.

Nor is notice to a policeman, unless he be an agent or servant of the city ; and he is not so in Troy.

Kunz v. Troy, 36 Hun, 615.
[Rev. 5 N. Y. St. R. 642, but on other points.]

Nor in Buffalo.

McKay *v.* Buffalo, 9 Hun, 401 ; 74 N. Y. 619.

But is in New York.

Rehberg *v.* New York, 91 N. Y. 137.
Twogood *v.* New York, 102 N. Y. 216.

[For other cases on this point, see page 120, *ante.*

B. CONSTRUCTIVE NOTICE.

1. Rule. *Constructive notice is proven by showing that the defect or obstruction causing the injury had existed so long and under such circumstances before the injury that the agents of the city actually knew, or, in the exercise of reasonable diligence, should have known it.*

2. Notoriety. This inference of notice may be derived from its notoriety,—the knowledge of many citizens being strong evidence of notice to the city.

Bill *v.* Norrick, 39 Conn. 222.

And notoriety may be shown by any witness cognizant of the defect ; residents of the place or locality are not necessary.

Varnham *v.* Council Bluffs, 52 Iowa, 698.

For the purpose of showing notoriety, it is competent to prove who passed along the street, how frequently, and how employed ; and to that end it was held not incompetent to admit evidence of the patrolling of a street by police.

Kinney *v.* Troy, 38 Hun, 285.

3. Length of time. The length of time the defect had existed before the injury is always important, and may be shown by parol evidence, and by photographs, measurements and models.

Quinlan v. Utica, 11 Hun, 217; 74 N. Y. 603.

In practice, especially in icy-sidewalk cases, the continuous icy condition for such a time as to charge the city with constructive negligence is hard to prove, and also hard to rebut.

In such cases, where the condition is apt to be constantly changing by variations of temperature, great care must be taken to show, as nearly as may be, a continuous icy condition for as long a time as possible before the injury.

And it is proper to reject evidence of such condition at any particular time,—for example, a week before,— unless it is shown to have continued.

Woodcock v. Worcester, 138 Mass. 268.

4. Weather records. The condition of the weather preceding the injury is often important, for the purpose of determining the probable continuous existence of the ice ; and this is conveniently and frequently shown by the record of persons employed to take meteorological observations by the United States signal service.

These were declared competent evidence, and reasons given therefor in

Evanston v. Gunn, 99 U. S. 660.

5. **Other accidents.** One way of establishing the fact of continuous obstruction is, by proving that others had fallen or sustained injury at the same place, and prior to the injury in suit.

> Burns *v.* Schenectady, 24 Hun, 10.
> Avery *v.* Syracuse, 29 Hun, 537.
> Champlin *v.* Penu Yan, 34 Hun, 33.
> Quinlan *v.* Utica, 11 Hun, 217 ; 74 N. Y. 603.
> Dist. Col. *v.* Armes, 107 U. S. 519.
> Delphi *v.* Lowery, 74 Ind. 520.
> Smith *v.* Sherwood, (Mich.) 34 A. L. J. 119.
> Chicago *v.* Powers, 42 Ill. 169.
> Augusta *v.* Hafers, 61 Ga. 48.
> Darling *v.* Westmoreland, 52 N. H. 401.
> Kent *v.* Lincoln, 32 Vt. 591.

Yet such fact alone does not establish that the obstruction was actionable.

> Dubois *v.* Kingston, 102 N. Y., 219.

In O'Hagan *v.* Dillon, 76 N. Y. 170, where evidence of the recovery of a judgment for another injury at the same place was rejected, there was no issue of notice, the action being against the persons who caused the obstruction.

6. **Ordinances.** The existence of an ordinance directing how vault-covers shall be placed, held not evidence of knowledge on the part of city, that if the provisions of the ordinance were not observed, there would be danger of slipping on the vault-covers.

> Stillwell *v.* New York, 49 Super. 360.

Nor is a city responsible for the failure of householders to obey its ordinances.

> Taylor *v.* Yonkers, 26 W. Dig. 376.

CHAPTER VII.

CONTRIBUTORY NEGLIGENCE.

1. Burden on plaintiff.
2. Rule in many States.
3. New York rule.
4. Circumstances.
5. Evidence necessary.
6. Wrongful act.

1. Burden on plaintiff. It seems to be the almost universally recognized rule in this State that in negligence cases the proof of absence of contributory negligence is essential to the plaintiff's recovery.

Riceman *v.* Havemeyer, 84 N. Y. 647.
Hale *v.* Smith, 78 N. Y. 480.
Lehman *v.* Brooklyn, 29 Barb. 234.
Delafield *r.* Union Ferry Co., 10 Bosw. 216.
Cordell *v.* N. Y. C., &c. R. R. Co., 75 N. Y. 330.
Hart *v.* Hudson R. Br. Co., 80 N. Y. 622.
Glendening *v.* Sharp, 22 Hun, 78.
Kenney *v.* N. Y. & Manhattan Beach R. R. Co., 13 W. Dig. 61.
Halpin *v.* Third Ave. R. R. Co., 40 Super. 175.
McMahon *v.* N. Y. El. R. R. Co., 50 Super. 507.
Schindler *v.* N. Y., L. E. & W. R. R. Co., 1 N. Y. St. R. 289.
Warner *r.* N. Y. C. R. R. Co., 44 N. Y. 465.
Hoag *v.* N. Y. C., &c. R. R. Co., 21 W. Dig. 506.

And the same rule applies in Maine,

> Benson v. Titcomb, 72 Me. 31.
> Merrill v. North Yarmouth, 3 Atl. R. 575.

and in Vermont,

> Bovee v. Danville, 53 Vt. 183.

Michigan,

> Mich. Cent. R. R. Co. v. Coleman, 28 Mich. 440.

and Massachusetts.

> Mayo v. Boston, &c. R. R., 104 Mass. 137.

2. Rule in many States. A different rule seems to be adopted in many States, and in the United States courts. namely : that the burden of proving contributory negligence is upon the party charging it; and there can be no nonsuit upon that ground unless the plaintiff's case discloses such negligence.

> Hobson v. New Mexico, &c. Ry. Co., (Arizona) 11
>　. Pac. R. 545.
> McDougall v. Cent. P. R. R. Co., 63 Cal. 431.
> Sanders v. Reister, 1 Dakota Ter. 151.
> Cincinnati, &c. R. R. Co. v. Butler, (Indiana) 2
>　No. East. Rep. 138.
> Frech v. Philadelphia, &c. R. R. Co., 39 Md. 574.
> County Com'rs v. Burgess, (Md) 30 Alb. L. J. 79.
> Hocum v. Weitherick, 22 Minn. 152.
> Buesching v. St. Louis Gaslight Co., 73 Mo. 219.
> Lincoln v. Walker, (Nebraska) 30 Alb. L. J. 406.
> Penn. Canal Co. v. Bentley, 66 Pa. St. 30.
> Cleveland, &c. R. R. Co. v. Rowan, Id. 393.
> Dallas, &c. Ry. Co. v. Spicker, 61 Tex. 427.
> Hoyt v. Hudson, 41 Wis. 104.
> R. R. Co. v. Gladmon, 15 Wall. 401.

The same doctrine was held in New York, in

> Robinson r. New York Central, &c. R. R. Co., 65 Barb. 146.

Affirmed, 66 N. Y. 11; but without passing upon this point, and in no other case.

> (See Article, 20 Alb. L. J. 304, discussing the rule in different States.)

3. **The New York rule,** as stated above, is modified in its application, into a rule which involves a somewhat metaphysical distinction, and is well stated in the head-note to Button v. Hudson River R. R. Co., 18 N. Y. 248.

" In an action for negligence, the burden is upon the plaintiff to prove affirmatively that he is guiltless of any negligence proximately contributing to the injury. Such negligence is not to be presumed, and therefore direct evidence to disprove it is not required from the plaintiff in the first instance ; but where there is conflicting testimony as to the facts, the preponderance must be with the plaintiff, to enable him to recover."

In that case the court say : " It must not be understood that it was incumbent on the plaintiff, in the first instance, to give evidence for the direct and special object of establishing the observance of due care by the intestate ; it would be enough if the proof introduced of the negligence of the defendants and the circumstances of the injury, *prima facie*, established that the injury was occasioned by the negligence of the defendants ; as such evidence would exclude the idea of a want of due care by the intestate aiding to the result. . . . The fact must appear in same way, but in what particular mode, is unimportant. The evidence of it may be direct and positive, or only circumstantial."

4. **Circumstances.** Other cases holding that the absence of contributory negligence may be inferred from circumstances, are the following :

> Nowell v. New York, 52 Super. 382.
> Fitzgerald v. Binghamton, 40 Hun, 332.
> Johnson v. H. R. R. R. Co., 20 N. Y. 65.
> Smedis v. B. & R. B. R. R. Co., 23 Hun, 279 ; 88 N. Y. 13.
> Moody v. Osgood, 54 N. Y. 488.
> Morrison r. N.Y. C. & H. R. R. R. Co., 63 N.Y. 643.
> Hart v. Hudson River Br. Co., 84 N. Y. 56.
> Jones r. N. Y. C., &c. R. R. Co., 10 Abb. N. C. 200; aff. 28 Hun, 364; 92 N. Y. 628.
> Schwandner v. Birge, 33 Hun, 186.

To the same effect in other States.

> Mayo v. Boston, &c. R. R. Co., 104 Mass. 137.
> Chicago, &c. R. R. Co. v. Clark, 108 Ill. 113.
> Texas, &c. Ry. Co. v. Crowder, 63 Tex. 502.
> New Jersey Exp. Co. v. Nichols, 33 N. J. L. 434.

Among the circumstances which have been held sufficient to raise the inference of care on the part of the plaintiff, may be mentioned the following :

(a) Character of defendant's negligence, which may be such as *prima facie* to establish the whole issue.

> Johnson v. H. R. R. R. Co., *supra.*

(b) Known indisposition of men needlessly to subject themselves to danger.

> Id.
> Schwandner v. Birge, *supra.*

(c) In case of injury causing death, there being no witnesses of the injury, the habits of the deceased as to sobriety, prudence, &c.

> Chicago, &c. R. R. Co. v. Clark, *supra.*
> *Contra*, Chase v. Maine Cent. R. R. Co.. 77 Me. 62.

(d) The absence of all appearance of fault.

> Mayo v. Boston, &c. R. R., *supra.*

(e) Person found dead at the foot of wall, above which was a street unguarded ; last seen alone on street above.

> Nowell v. New York, *supra.*

(f) Fact that plaintiff was injured in the night-time, while engaged in the discharge of his duty as a brakeman on defendants' train, by the breaking of a ladder attached to his car.

> Jones *s.* New York Central & H. R. R. R. Co., *supra.*

5. **There must**, however, be some evidence as to the conduct of the injured person.

> Glendening v. Sharp, 22 Hun, 78.

And where circumstances point as much to contributory negligence as to its absence, or in neither direction, there can be no recovery.

> Kenney v. Manhattan B. R. R. Co., 13 W. Dig. 61.
> Tolman v. Syracuse, &c. R. R. Co., 98 N. Y. 198.
> McDermott r. Third Ave. R. R. Co., 26 W. Dig. 250.

6. **For wrongful act.** It may be added here, that where .

14

the injury was caused by wrongful act rather than negligence, the burden of proving contributory negligence is on the defendant.

Clifford *v.* Dam, 81 N. Y. 52.
McGuire *v.* Spence, 91 N. Y. 303.

CHAPTER VIII.

DAMAGES.

THE fact of injury is of course the chief requisite in

the line of proof ; its extent is important to be shown only upon the question of damages. For convenience, both fact and extent are considered under the general subject of damages. Some classes of evidence which have been held proper to lay before the jury, to enable them to fix the amount of recovery, in case they find for the plaintiff, will be given under the somewhat arbitrary classification which follows :

A.   ACTION BY PERSON INJURED.

1. **Fact of injury.** This may be proven by the direct evidence of the person injured.

Also by others present, that the plaintiff made exclamations of pain at the time of the injury.

> Hagenlocher r. C. I. & B. R. R. Co., 99 N. Y. 136.
> Nichols v. Brooklyn City R. R. Co., 30 Hun, 437.
> Elkhart v. Ritter, 66 Ind. 136.

Also by physicians who attended the injured person, or otherwise made examination.

The physician may testify to the extent of the injury, judging from his examination, including what the patient said at the time, and the indications of suffering, although there was no external evidence of injury.

> Quaife v. Chicago, &c., Ry. Co., 48 Wis. 513.

Examination eight months after injury, held too remote.

> Mosher r. Russell, 26 W. Dig. 234.

Plaintiff may exhibit the injured member to the jury.

> Jordan v. Bowen, 46 Super. 355.
> Hiller v. Sharon Springs, 28 Hun, 344.
> Indiana Car Co. v. Parker. 100 Ind. 181.

But cannot be compelled to do so by order before trial.

Roberts *v.* Ogdensburgh, &c. R. R. Co., 29 Hun, 154.
Newman *v.* Third Ave. R. R. Co., 19 W. Dig. 500.

An examination in court by a physician in behalf of the defendant was held properly denied.

Archer *v.* Sixth Ave. R. R. Co., 52 Super. 378.

2. Speculative injury. *Consequences of an injury from negligence which are contingent, speculative, or merely possible, are not proper to be considered in estimating the damages, and may not be proved.*

Strohm *v.* N. Y., &c. R. R. Co., 96 N. Y. 305.
Walrath *v.* Whittekind, 26 Kan. 482.
Tozer *v.* N. Y. C., &c. R. R. Co., 26 W. Dig. 72.

2. Measure of damages, generally. *Damages for personal injury include everything of which the plaintiff has been deprived as a direct and natural consequence of the injury.*

Huizega *v.* Cutler, &c. Lumber Co., 51 Mich. 272.

4. Compensatory only. *For mere negligence, punitive damages cannot be recovered. Only compensatory damages can be allowed.*

Wilson *v.* Granby, 47 Conn. 59.
Burr *v.* Plymouth, 48 Conn. 460.
Chicago *v.* Langlass, 52 Ill. 256.
Chicago *v.* Kelly, 69 Ill. 475.
Louisville, &c. Ry. Co. *v.* Shanks, 94 Ind. 598.
Parsons *v.* Lindsay, 26 Kan. 426.
Wilson *v.* Wheeling, 19 W. Va. 323.

5. Prospective damages. *The person injured can have but one action for such injury, and in that action he may have prospective damages.*

> Filer *v.* New York Central R. R. Co., 49 N. Y. 42.
> Elkhart *v.* Ritter, 66 Ind. 136.
> Weisenberg *v.* Appleton, 26 Wis. 56.
> Staal *v.* Grand St., &c. R. R. Co., 36 Hun, 208.
> Wardle *v.* New Orleans City R. R. Co., 35 La. An.
>   202.
> Secord *v.* St. Paul, &c. Ry. Co., 18 Fed. R. 221.
> Scott *v.* Montgomery, 95 Pa. St. 444.
> Chicago, &c. R. R. Co. *v.* Avery, 10 Ill. Ap. 210.
> Matteson *v.* New York Central R. R. Co., 62 Barb.
>   364, 35 N. Y. 487.
> Aaron *v.* Second Ave. R. R. Co., 2 Daly, 127.
> Houston, &c. Ry. Co. *v* Boehm, 57 Tex. 152.
> Klein *v.* Jewett, 36 N. J. Eq. 474.
> McLaughlin *v.* Corry, 77 Pa. St., 109.
> Stafford *v.* Oskaloosa, 64 Iowa, 251.

The limit in respect to future damages is, that they must be such as it is reasonably certain will inevitably and necessarily result from the injury.

> Filer *v.* N. Y. C. R. R. Co., *supra.*
> Stafford *v.* Oskaloosa, *supra.*
> Marvin *v.* Manhattan Ry. Co., 53 Super. 527.

For the purpose of estimating future damages, physicians may be sworn as to the probable result of the injury.

> Wendell *v.* Troy, 39 Barb. 329; 4 Abb. Dec. 563.
> Strohm *v.* N. Y., &c. R. R. Co., 96 N. Y. 305.
> Jones *v.* Utica, &c. R. R. Co., 40 Hun, 349.
> Griswold *v.* N.Y. Cent., &c. R. R. Co., 26 W. Dig. 358.

6. Direct pecuniary loss. *This may include expenses attending illness, such as physicians', druggists' and nurses' bills ;* (¹) *also value of time lost.* (²)

(¹) Giblin *r*. McIntyre, 2 Utah, 384.
   Sheehan *v*. Edgar, 58 N. Y. 631.
   Metcalf *r*. Baker, 57 N. Y. 662.
   So. & No. Anna R. R. Co. *r*. McLendon, 63 Ala. 266.
   Reed *r*. Chicago, &c. R. R. Co., 57 Iowa, 23.
   Brignoli *r*. Chicago, &c. Ry. Co., 4 Daly, 182.
(²) Nones *r*. Northouse, 46 Vt. 587.
   Metcalf *r*. Baker, *supra*.
   Drinkwater *r*. Dinsmore, 16 Hun, 250.
   Rev'd on other grounds, 80 N. Y. 390.

But board cannot be allowed.

> Graiber *r*. Derwin, 43 Cal. 495.

These may be both accrued and prospective.

> Stall *v*. Grand St., &c. R. R. Co., 36 Hun, 208.
> Scott *v*. Montgomery, 95 Pa. St. 444.
> Houston, &c. Ry. Co. *v*. Boehm, 57 Tex. 152.
> Drinkwater *v*. Dinsmore, *supra*.
> Brignoli *v*. Chicago, &c. Ry. Co., *supra*.
> Chicago, &c. R. R. Co. *v*. Avery, 10 Ill. Ap. 210.
> McLaughlin *v*. Corry, 77 Pa. St. 109.

Upon the question of accrued expense, the jury cannot speculate. Nothing can be allowed therefor, unless the amount be shown or facts from which to estimate it.

Thus of value of lost time,

> Leeds *r*. Metropolitan Gas L. Co., 90 N. Y. 26.

and of medicines and attendance.

> Reed *r*. Chicago, &c. R. R. Co., 57 Iowa, 23.
> Eckerd *r*. Chicago, etc. Ry. Co., (Iowa) 30 No. W. R. 615.

It has been held, in New York and Illinois, that the amount paid for medical attendance cannot be allowed without proof that the plaintiff paid it or became liable therefor.

> Drinkwater *v.* Dinsmore, 80 N. Y. 390.
> Moody *v.* Osgood, 50 Barb. 626.
> Joliet *v.* Henry, 11 Ill. Ap. 154.
> Chicago *v.* Honey, 10 Ill. Ap. 535.

But in several States the value of services of physicians and nurses is held to be properly shown, though it was gratuitous.

> Klein *v.* Thompson, 19 Ohio St. 569.
> Penn Co., &c. *v.* Marion, (Ind.) 3 No. East Rep. 874.
> Varnham *v.* Council Bluffs, 52 Iowa, 698.

Damages may be given for future expenses, even if there be no proof as to the past.

> Staal *v.* Grand St., &c. R. R. Co., 36 Hun, 208.

7. **Evidence of loss.** For the purpose of proving pecuniary loss, both past and future, the following evidence has been held competent.

Inability to attend to business.

> Indianapolis *v.* Gaston, 58 Ind. 224.
> Walker *v.* Erie Ry. Co., 63 Barb. 260.
> Brignoli *v.* Chicago, &c. Ry. Co., 4 Daly, 182.

That sole means of support was earnings as physician.

> Stafford *v.* Oskaloosa, 64 Iowa, 251.

Past earnings and capacity to earn.

> Ehrgott *v.* New York, 96 N. Y. 264.
> Nash *v.* Sharpe, 19 Hun, 365.
> Simonin *v.* N. Y., &c. R. R. Co., 36 Hun, 214.
> Louisville, &c. Ry. Co. *v.* Frawley, (Ind.) 9 No.
>   E. R. 594.

Difference of earnings before and after injury.

> Conner *v.* Pioneer, &c. Co., 29 Fed. R. 629.

8. Speculative damages. *Prospective profits in business are not usually recoverable, being in their nature speculative.*

> Phyfe r. Manhattan Ry. Co., 30 Hun, 377.
> Marks r. L. I. R. R. Co., 25 W. Dig. 189.

And in such case past profits are incompetent to prove them.

> Masterton r. Mt. Vernon, 58 N. Y. 391.

Upon the same principle it has been held incompetent to show that the plaintiff was in line of promotion, and expected to receive greater wages.

> Brown r. Chicago, &c. R. R. Co., 64 Iowa, 652.

9. Double damages. *One cannot recover for his own loss of time and capacity to labor, and also what he had to pay another to supply that loss of labor.*

> Blackman r. Gardiner Bridge, 75 Me. 214.

10. Physical and mental sufferings, *both present and future, are proper elements of damages.*

> Ransom r. N. Y. & E. R. R. Co., 15 N. Y. 415.
> Curtis r. R. & Syr. R. R. Co., 18 N. Y. 534.
> Walker r. Erie Ry. Co., 63 Barb. 260.
> So. & No. Anna R. R. Co. r. McLendon, 23 Ala. 266.
> Drinkwater r. Dinsmore, 16 Hun, 250.
> De Forest r. Utica, 69 N. Y. 614.
> Giblin r. McIntyre, 2 Utah, 384.
> Porter r. Hannibal, &c. R. R. Co., 71 Mo. 66.
> Hamilton r. Third Ave. R. R. Co., 40 Super. 376.

To which may be added "consequent privation and inconvenience."

> Scott *r*. Montgomery, 95 Pa. St. 444.
> McLaughlin *v*. Corry, 77 Id. 109.

Mental suffering, however, does not constitute a distinct item of damages.

> Giblin *v*. McIntyre, *supra*.
> Salina *v*. Trosper, 27 Kan. 544.

The pain and suffering resulting from the plaintiff's
want of care in seeking recovery cannot be considered.

> Gilman *v*. Haley, 7 Ill. Ap. 349.

Nor his anxiety for the safety of others.

> Keyes *v*. Minneapolis Ry. Co. (Minn.), 30 N. W. R.
> 888.

11. Disease contracted. *Injury to health is a proper subject
of inquiry.*

> Beckwith *v*. New York Central R. R. Co., 64 Barb.
> 299.

And if disease resulted from the injury, damages may be
allowed for it.

> Houston, &c. Ry. Co. *v*. Leslie, 57 Tex. 83.
> Stewart *v*. Ripon, 38 Wis. 584.
> Baltimore, &c. Ry. Co. *v*. Kemp, (Md.) 30 Alb. L.
> J. 90.
> Ehrgott *v*. New York, 96 N. Y. 264.
> Oliver *v*. La Valle, 36 Wis. 592.

12. Ill-health before injury. *If by reason of a delicate
condition of health the consequences of a negligent injury are
more serious still, for those consequences the defendant is liable,
although they were aggravated by the imperfect bodily condition.*

> Tice *v*. Munn, 94 N. Y. 621.
> Louisville, &c. Ry. Co. *v*. Jones, (Ind.) 9 No. East.
> R. 476.

13. Pecuniary condition. Evidence of the wealth or poverty of the plaintiff,(¹) or his family,(²) or the defendant,(³) is incompetent in several States.

(¹) Shea r. Potrero, &c. R. R. Co., 44 Cal. 414.
Eagle Packet Co. r. Defries, 94 Ill. 598.
La Salle v. Thorndike, 7 Ill. Ap. 282.
Missouri Pac. R. R. Co. r. Lyde, 57 Tex. 505.
(²) Chicago v. O'Brennan, 65 Ill. 160.
Louisville, &c. Co. r. Gower, (Tenn) 3 So. W. R. 824.
(³) Chicago City Ry. Co. r. Henry, 62 Ill. 142.

14. Married woman. *A wife can recover only for such loss of services as she has sustained herself and towards herself.*

Minick r. Troy, 19 Hun, 253; 83 N. Y. 514.

She may, however, testify that she did all the work for her husband and large family.

Joliet r. Conway, (Ill.) 10 No. East. R. 223.

She may recover for inability to care for her property [her husband being a cripple].

Fitzsimons r. Rome, 21 W. Dig. 343.

Formerly it was held that a married woman could not recover for expenses of medical attendance, unless she had charged her separate estate with its payment.

Moody r. Osgood, 50 Barb. 628.

B. ACTION BY HUSBAND OR PARENT.

1. Measure of damages to husband. *The measure of damages to a husband whose wife has been injured by negligence, is* *the value of her services and his reasonable expenses in procuring necessary treatment and care for her.*

> Meigs r. Buffalo, 23 W. Dig. 497.

The husband may recover for the necessary labor substituted for the ordinary service of his wife, and for his own services in attending her.

> Lindsey r. Danville, 46 Vt. 144.

And for loss of her society.

> Jones v. Utica & Black River R. R. Co., 40 Hun, 349.

This may be both present and prospective ; and a physician may testify to the natural and probable duration of the injury.

> Jones r. U. & B. R. R. R. Co., *supra.*

2. Measure of damages to parent. This is the same as in the last case, except that in estimating prospective damages the question for the jury to determine is how far the injuries are permanent as affecting the ability of the child to work until its majority.

> Hussey v. Ryan, (Md.) 4 East. R. 462.

C. For Injury Causing Death.

1. Introductory. The cause of action, where one exists, where injuries from negligence are the cause of death, being, as stated in Part I. chapter II., wholly statutory, and the law and practice thereon being different in different States, it is difficult to formulate any general rules.

The New York statutes are given at pages 14 to 18, and attention will be mainly confined to the rules and decisions under those statutes.

2. New York rule. The New York rule gives the cause of action for the "benefit of the husband or wife and next of kin "; and provides that the damages awarded shall be, within the limit established, "a fair and just compensation for the pecuniary injuries resulting from the decedent's death to the person or persons for whose benefit the action is brought."

3. Pecuniary damage. The first principle to be observed under this and similar statutes is that:—*The recovery must be confined to the pecuniary loss sustained by the death of the intestate; and damages can be only awarded on proof of such loss.*

> Mitchell *v.* New York Central, &c. R. R. Co., 2 Hun, 535 ; 64 N. Y. 655.

But proof of slight loss will warrant submission to the jury.

> Cornwall *v.* Mills, 44 N. Y. Super. 45.

The jury must, however, judge, not guess.

> Houghkirk *v.* Delaware & Hudson C. Co., 92 N.Y. 219.

There can be no allowance for grief or bereavement of the survivors.

> Lebman *v.* Brooklyn, 29 Barb. 234.
> Tilley *v.* Hudson River R. R. Co., 24 N. Y. 471.
> Etherington *v.* P. P. & C. I. R. R. Co., 88 N. Y. 641.
> Galveston *v.* Barbour, 62 Tex. 172.
> Mansfield, &c. Co. *v.* McEnery, 91 Pa. St. 185.
> Huntingdon, &c. R. R. Co. *v.* Decker, 84 Id. 419.
> Kansas Pacific Ry. Co. *v.* Cutter, 19 Kan. 83.

Nashville, &c. R. R. Co. v. Stevens, (Tenn.) 9 Heisk.
12.

Contra. Baltimore, &c. R. R. Co. v. Noell, (Virginia) 32
Gratt. 394.

Owen v. Brockschmidt, 54 Mo. 285.

Nor for loss of society and companionship.

Lehman v. Brooklyn, *supra*.
Etherington v. P. P., &c. R. R. Co , *supra*.
Howard Co. Comrs. v. Legg, 93 Ind. 523.

4. Loss to beneficiaries only. *Damages can be awarded only for the loss to the persons provided for in the statute.*

There can be none for the personal wrong or suffering of the person killed.

Tilley v. Hudson River R. R. Co., 24 N. Y. 471.
Etherington v. P. P., &c. R. R Co., 88 N. Y. 641.
Holton v. Daly, 106 Ill. 131.

Or for his expense for medical treatment.

Holton v. Daly, *supra*.

Unless a beneficiary is chargeable with it, in which case it is a proper item.

Murphy v. N. Y. C., &c. R. R. Co., 88 N. Y. 445.
Pennsylvania R. R. Co. v. Bantom, 54 Pa. St. 495.
Roeder v. Ormsby, 22 How. Pr. 270.

5. Actual and prospective. *Both special or actual and prospective general damages may be allowed.*

Houghkirk v. D. & H. Canal Co., 92 N. Y. 219.
Gumb v. Twenty-third St. R. R. Co., 1 N. Y. St.
R. 715.

The beneficiary will not be limited to nominal damages, though there be no positive evidence of actual pecuniary loss.

> Dickens *v.* New York Central R. R. Co., 1 Abb. Dec. 504.
> Ryall *v.* Kennedy, 40 Super. 347.
> Kennedy *v.* Ryall, 67 N. Y. 379.

Thus in action for killing a young child.

> Prendegast *v.* New York Central, &c. R. R. Co., 58 N. Y. 652.
> Gorham *v.* New York Central, &c. R. R. Co., 23 Hun, 449.

But when special damages are sought, their character and amount should be proven.

> Houghkirk *v.* D. & H. Canal Co., *supra.*

6. Measure of general damages. *The basis of general damages in case of death by negligence is the reasonable expectation of pecuniary advantage for the continuance of the life.*

> Thomas *v.* U. & B. R. R. R. Co., 6 Civ. Pro. R. 353 ; 34 Hun, 626 ; 98 N. Y. 649.
> Burton *v.* Wilmington, &c. R. R. Co., 82 N. C. 504.
> Mansfield Coal, &c. Co. *v.* McEnery, 91 Pa. St. 185.
> Collins *v.* Davidson, 19 Fed. R. 83.
> Nashville, &c. R. R. Co. *v.* Stovens, 9 Heisk. (Tenn.) 12.
> Rafferty *v.* Buckman, 46 Iowa, 195.
> Carpenter *v.* Buffalo, &c. R. R. Co., 38 Hun, 116.

7. Elements and evidence of same. Pecuniary injuries

may be such as arise from the loss of personal care, intellectual culture or moral training.

> McIntyre *v.* N. Y. C., &c. R. R. Co., 37 N. Y. 287.
> Tilley *v.* H. R. R. R. Co., 24 N. Y. 471.

The probable duration of life is a question to be considered.

> Scheffler *v.* Minneapolis, &c. Ry. Co., 32 Minn. 518.

This may be shown by the Northampton tables.

> Sauter *v.* New York Central, &c. R. R. Co., 66 N
> Y. 50.

It is proper to consider the age, sex,([1]) character, qualities, capacity and condition ;([2]) business, property and pecuniary prospects ;([3]) age, habits, industry, means, business ;([4]) age, ability, disposition to work, habits of living and expenditure ;([5]) general character for industry and kindness (but not specific acts); ([6]) usual earnings ([7]) of the decedent.

> ([1]) Ihl *v.* Forty-second St. R. R. Co., 47 N. Y. 317.
> ([2]) Lockwood *v.* N. Y., L. E., &c. R. R. Co., 98 N. Y.
> 523.
> ([3]) Kansas Pac. Ry. Co. *v.* Cutter, 19 Kan. 83.
> Huntingdon, &c. R. R. Co. *v.* Decker, 84 Pa. St.
> 419.
> March *v.* Walker, 48 Tex. 372.
> ([4]) Burton *v.* Wilmington, &c. R. R. Co., 82 N. C. 504.
> ([5]) Mansfield Coal, &c. Co. *v.* McEnery, 91 Pa. St. 185.
> ([6]) Quinn *v.* Power, 29 Hun, 183.
> Reversed on other grounds, 87 N. Y. 535.
> ([7]) McIntyre *v.* N. Y. C. R. R., &c. Co., 37 N. Y. 287.

It is also proper to show the age, sex, circumstances and condition of the next of kin.

Lockwood *r.* New York, &c. R. R. Co., 98 N. Y.
523.
Ihl *r.* Forty-second St. R. R. Co., 47 N. Y. 319.
Carpenter *r.* Buffalo, &c. R. R. Co., 38 Hun, 116.

In Indiana (¹) and Illinois (²) it is held, that the pecuniary condition of those who would benefit by the recovery cannot be shown.

(¹) Mayhew *r.* Burns, 2 No. East. Rep. 793.
   Indianapolis, &c. Ry. Co. *v.* Pitzer, 6 No. East.
   Rep. 310.
(²) Chicago *r.* McCulloch, 10 Ill. Ap. 459.
   Chicago, &c. Ry. Co. *v.* Moranda, 93 Ill. 302.
   Chicago, &c. R. R. Co. *v.* Henry, 7 Ill. Ap. 322.

The fact cannot be considered that the plaintiff as
next of kin of the decedent is entitled to her property (¹)
or life-insurance.(²)

(¹) Terry *r.* Jewett, 78 N. Y. 338.
   Malonee *v.* N. Y. C., &c. R. R. Co., 20 W. Dig. 252.
   Chicago, &c. Ry. Co. *v.* Bayfield, 37 Mich. 205.
(²) Kellogg *v.* N. Y. C., &c. R. R. Co., 79 N. Y. 73.

8. Damages to parent. *Where the father sues as administrator and is the sole beneficiary, he may recover all the
damages which he would have been entitled to had his son survived the injury.*

McGovern *r.* N. Y. C., &c. R. R. Co., 67 N. Y. 417.
Stuebing *r.* Marshall, 2 Civ. Pro. 77.

This includes cost of nursing and medical attendance,
and funeral expenses.

Rains *v.* St. Louis, &c. Ry. Co., 71 Mo. 164.

15

Also loss of services during minority.

> McGovern v. N. Y. C., &c. Co., *supra*.
> Gill v. R. & P. R. R. Co., 37 Hun, 107.
> Rains v. St. Louis, &c. Ry. Co., 71 Mo. 164.

From which must be deducted the probable cost of maintenance.

> Benton v. Chicago, &c. R. R. Co., 55 Iowa, 496.
> St. Louis, &c. Ry. Co. v. Freeman, 36 Ark. 41.

But loss of possible counsel and advice cannot be allowed.

> Gill v. R. & P. R. R. Co., *supra*.

The measure of value of a child's services is such as is ordinary with children in the same condition and station of life, without regard to any peculiar value the plaintiff might attach to the child's services.

> St. Louis, &c. Ry. Co. v. Freeman, *supra*.

The recovery in such case is not, however, limited to loss of services of the child during its minority; the action would still lie though the child were of age.

> Birkett v. Knickerbocker Ice Co., 25 W. Dig 46.
> Lockwood v. N. Y., &c. R. R. Co., *supra*.

Prospective damages for loss of services of a child cannot be recovered unless specially alleged.

> Gilligan v. N.Y. & Harlem R. R. Co., 1 E. D. Sm. 453.

9. Interest. In 1870 it was for the first time enacted in

New York that damages in such a case should draw interest from the time of death, the interest to be "added to the verdict and inserted in the entry of judgment."

Laws 1870, chap. 78.

Prior to that enactment it had been held, that while the jury might take into account the time that had elapsed as affecting the amount of damages, yet they could not agree upon a certain sum as damages, and add to it interest thereon from the time of death.

Cook *v.* New York Central, &c. R. R. Co., 10 Hun, 426.

And the Court of Appeals hold that the position of the jury is the same under the Act of 1870; and that where the jury had thus included interest in their verdict the clerk was still bound to add interest upon the entry of judgment.

Manning *v.* Pt. Henry Iron Co., 91 N. Y. 634.

It has been held that the rate of interest in a given case is regulated by the statute in force when the verdict was rendered.

Salter *v.* Utica, &c. R. R. Co., 86 N. Y. 401.
(Overruling Erwin *v.* Neversink, &c. Co., 23 Hun, 578.)

10. Summary. The whole subject of measure of damages in case death results from an injury caused by negligence, is excellently summed up in the opinion in Carpenter *v.* Buffalo, &c. R. R. Co., 38 Hun, 116, from which the following is quoted :

"The estimate of them does not necessarily depend upon the pecuniary condition of the next of kin as distinguished from the loss suffered, nor are they dependent upon a legal duty or obligation of the deceased during the time of his life or in the future, if he had continued to live.

"While the injury must be pecuniary merely, and the damages ascertained from the evidence, their sources may not be in the loss, impairment or destruction of any established legal right, but in the deprivation of what reasonably may be, or may have been, expected by those for whose benefit the recovery is had, from the continuance of the life of the deceased. Nor are they confined to the present loss or injury, but may include such as the jury may upon the evidence believe and find will in the future result from the death as the proximate cause of it. The prospective injuries may be in the loss of aid, care and attention, whether by services and money, or either, and by advice, direction and protection, or either, in business, whether for purposes of accumulation or preservation of the estate of the next of kin. In fact, 'the statute has set no bounds to the sources of those pecuniary injuries.'

"There may be difficulty in finding support for the estimates made, in any well-defined rule of reasoning or in the logic of the facts presented by the evidence, but that is usually for the jury to demonstrate by their verdict only, in finding which they are required to keep within the limit, in respect to amount, prescribed by the statute.

"These damages are found in the natural and rational consequences which in the judgment of the jury have resulted, and may, and therefore will, result to the next of kin, when such alone are the sufferers of those named in the statute as the beneficiaries of the recovery.

"They are not susceptible of direct proof, and no evidence of actual injury is necessary to support an action, other than such as may show the relation and situation of those who may be entitled to the fruits of the remedy. The amount of recovery is dependent much on the ability of the deceased in his lifetime, or that which he might, if living, possess in future; hence his mental and physical qualities are properly matters for consideration, as well as his particular relations to those for whose benefit relief is sought. And out of the uncertainty of the pecuniary advantages which his life might have afforded to them, the jury are to find certainty to a reasonable extent in the evidence in support of their judgment of the pecuniary injury sustained."

CHAPTER IX.

1. Generally. The defendant may, of course, rebut all the facts which the plaintiff attempts to establish. Thus, it may offer evidence to disprove the facts of incorporation and duty to repair (though an action is hardly presumable where these elements are not beyond dispute), and the fact that the place of the accident was upon one of its streets ; may dispute the fact and amount of injury ; may deny the existence of the defect or obstruction ; may deny that it had notice or was negligent ; may attempt to prove contributory negligence of the plaintiff; may offer evidence to reduce the amount of damages. It is only purposed to notice some decisions upon what may and what may not prevent a recovery by the plaintiff.

2. Evidence to rebut negligence. (a) A city may prove

[230]

that a guard placed at an excavation was removed by a stranger.

> Sevestre *v.* New York, 47 Super. 341.
> Parker *v.* Cohoes, 10 Hun, 531; 74 N. Y. 610.
> Doherty *v.* Waltham, 4 Gray, 596.
> Mullen *v.* Rutland, 55 Vt. 77.
> Klatt *v.* Milwaukee, 53 Wis. 196.

(b) It may also show the efforts it has made to keep the streets safe (¹) and the limitation of its power ; and to that end may show the extent of its streets, the amount of travel, the number of similar dangers, and its facilities for removing obstructions. (²)

> (¹) Tinkham *v.* New York, N. Y. Daily Reg., Oct. 22, 1883.
> (²) Reed *v.* New York, 31 Hun, 311.

(c) The absence of necessary funds and of legal means to procure them will excuse the neglect, but must be shown as a defense.

> Hines *v.* Lockport, 50 N. Y. 236.
> Weed *v.* Ballston, 76 N. Y. 329.

A city cannot raise the question that it is already indebted to an amount exceeding the constitutional limitation.

> Bloomington *v.* Perdue, 99 Ill. 329.

(d) It cannot excuse its negligence by showing that there were similar (¹) or worse (²) places in the neighborhood,

> (¹) Schoonmaker *v.* Wilbraham, 110 Mass. 134.
> Bauer *v.* Indianapolis, 99 Ind. 56.
> Temperance Hall As'n *v.* Giles, 33 N. J. L. 260.
> (²) Hyatt *v.* Rondout, 44 Barb. 385; 41 N. Y. 619.

or that others had passed uninjured.

Same cases.

(e) It cannot defend by showing that the defect existed at the time of incorporation, or the omission to make ordinances or by-laws in reference to repairing streets.

Nelson *v.* Cauisteo, 100 N. Y. 89.

(f) Legislative authority to make an excavation in a street does not authorize or excuse negligence in making it.

Steivermann *v.* White, 48 N. Y. Super. 523.

(g) The fact that a city has employed competent officers, does not excuse their negligence.

New York *v.* Furze, 3 Hill, 612.

(h) Nor can it excuse itself by laying the blame on an incompetent officer of its own selection.

Rochester, &c. Co. *v.* Rochester, 3 N. Y. 463.

(i) Nor by the fact that its officers believed the street to be safe.

Goodfellow *v.* New York, 100 N. Y. 15.

(j) Nor by instructing its subordinates to ascertain the facts and report.

Id.

(k) It cannot excuse itself by the fact that it has entered into a contract to repair the street.

Jacksonville *v.* Drew, 19 Fla. 106.

3. Notice. It is proper to show that those constantly using a street failed to notice the obstruction, as tending to the presumption that the municipal authorities had no notice.

> Broburg *v.* Des Moines, 63 Iowa, 523.

4. Act of plaintiff.

(a) As tending to show contributory negligence, it is proper to show that numerous persons passed on the same night without difficulty or danger.

> Fairbury *v.* Rogers, 2 Ill. App. 96.

(b) The ulterior purpose of the plaintiff in crossing a particular bridge, does not affect his right to have it safe.

> Strong *v.* Stevens Point, 62 Wis. 255.

(c) Nor is he barred because he was injured while doing an unlawful act,—as travelling on Sunday.

> Platz *v.* Cohoes, 89 N. Y. 219.
> Carroll *v.* S. I. R. R. Co., 58 N. Y. 126.
> Sutton *v.* Wauwatosa, 29 Wis. 21.
> Opsahl *v.* Judd, (Minn.) 27 Alb. L. J. 277.

5. Medical treatment. Unskillful treatment by physicians does not preclude from damages.

> Lyons *v.* Erie Ry. Co., 57 N. Y. 489.
> Tuttle *v.* Farmington, 58 N. H. 13.
> Pullman, &c. Co. *v.* Bluhm, 109 Ill. 20.

6. Predisposition to disease does not prevent a recovery.

> McNamara *v.* Clintonville, 62 Wis. 207.
> Baltimore City Ry. Co. *v.* Keefe, (Md.) 30 Alb.
> L. J. 90.

7. Damages. Undoubtedly, however, evidence of both the last two facts would be competent upon the question of damages.

So also the following :

(a) When the plaintiff claims to have been disabled from practicing as a physician, and claims damages therefor, held, that the defendant might show that this practice was unlawful; that he had no professional reputation.

> Jaques *v.* Bridgeport Horse R. R. Co., 41 Conn. 61.

(b) The defendant claiming upon a second trial that Bright's disease was caused by falling on a sidewalk, held, competent to show that no such claim had been made before.

> Freeport *v.* Isbell, 93 Ill. 381.

(c) Proof of loss of wages may be rebutted by showing that wages were really paid.

> Drinkwater *v.* Dinsmore, 80 N. Y. 390.

CHAPTER X.

1. Introductory. It has sometimes been said that the question of negligence in a particular case is one of mixed law and fact.

> Filer *v.* New York Central R. R. Co., 49 N. Y. 47.
> Greenleaf *v.* Illinois, &c. R. R. Co., 29 Iowa, 14.

Others pronounce it one of fact only.

> Thurber *v.* Harlem Bridge, &c. R. R. Co., 60 N. Y. 326.

The difference is one of expression ; the courts in the former cases meaning merely, as they say, that " it is the duty of the court to submit the same to the jury, with proper instructions as to the law."

The following seems to be the generally recognized general

2. Rule. *Where the evidence of negligence is undisputed or irresistible, it is for the court to decide; but where facts or inferences are in any way doubtful, the question of negligence is for the jury.*

> Cases cited under 1, *supra;* also,
> Gagg *v.* Vetter, 41 Ind. 228.
> Delaney *v.* Milwaukee, &c. R. R. Co., 33 Wis. 67.
> O'Neill *v.* Chicago, &c. Ry. Co., 1 McCrary C. Ct. 505.
> Hunt *v.* Salem, 121 Mass. 294.
> Payne *v.* Troy & Boston R. R. Co., 83 N. Y. 572.

The practical application of the above rule is suggested in the following:

Negligence is usually a question of fact. And especially so whenever men of ordinary prudence and discretion might differ as to the character of the act under the circumstances of the case.

> Hayes *v.* Miller, 70 N. Y. at p. 116.
> Thurber *v.* Harlem Br., &c. Ry. Co., 60 N. Y. at p. 331.
> Teipel *v.* Hilsendegen, 44 Mich. 461.

3. Illustrations. Each of the following questions have been held to be within the province of the jury:

(a) Whether a city is liable for injuries caused by the formation of ice around a pump and leader.

> Allison *v.* Middletown, 101 N. Y. 667.

(b) Whether a sidewalk is properly constructed.

> Sullivan *v.* Oshkosh, 55 Wis. 558.

(c) Whether a slight inequality, obstruction or depression is a dangerous defect.

Goodfel ow *v.* New York, 100 N. Y. 15.
Glantz *v.* So. Bend, (Ind.) 6 No. East. Rep. 632.

(d) Whether, after a snowfall, proper diligence is observed in making walks safe.

Providence *v.* Clapp, 17 How. (U. S.) 161.

(e) Whether a piece of gas apparatus fixed in a sidewalk so as to trip persons, is a defect for which the city is liable.

Loan *v.* Boston, 106 Mass. 450.

(f) Whether a city is responsible for a hole beside the sidewalk.

Phillips *v.* Fishkill, 26 W. Dig. 103.

(g) Or for a secret defect in an awning.

Humo *v.* New York, 47 N. Y. 639.

4. Contributory negligence ; rule. *To justify a non-suit on the ground of contributory negligence, the undisputed facts must show the omission or commission of some act which the law adjudges negligent ; the negligence must appear so clearly that no construction of the evidence or inference drawn from the facts will warrant a contrary conclusion.*

Stackus *v.* N. Y. C., &c. R. R. Co., 79 N. Y. 464.
Moody *v.* Osgood, 54 N. Y. 488.
Borst *v.* L. S. & M. S. Ry. Co., 4 Hun, 346 ; 66 N. Y. 639.
Munroe *v.* Third Ave. R. R. Co., 50 Super. 114.
Spaulding *v.* Jarvis, 32 Hun, 621.

Cook *v.* New York Central R. R. Co., 1 Abb. Dec.
432.
Osage City *v.* Brown, 27 Kan. 74.
Williams *v.* Syracuse Iron Works, 31 Hun, 392.
Pendril *v.* Second Ave. R. R. Co., 34 Super. 481.
Dickens *v.* New York Central R. R. Co., 1 Abb.
Dec. 504.
Rudolphy *v.* Fuchs, 44 How. Pr. 155.
Millard *v.* Pinard, 41 Vt. 34.
Pennsylvania R. R. Co. *v.* Righter, 42 N. J. L. 180.

5. **Contributory negligence, question for jury; cases.** The
cases in which the question of contributory negligence
has been decided to be for the jury to determine, are
very numerous.   Only a few will be mentioned, in which
municipal corporations were parties.

Diveny *v.* Elmira, 51 N. Y. 506.
Todd *v.* Troy, 61 N. Y. 506.
Niven *v.* Rochester, 76 N. Y. 619.
Sewell *v.* Cohoes, 75 N. Y. 45.
Gillespie *v.* Newburgh, 54 N. Y. 468.
Ruland *v.* South Newmarket, 59 N. H. 291.
Fassett *v.* Roxbury, 55 Vt. 552.
Shook *v.* Cohoes, 23 W. Dig. 4.

6. **When question of law.** (a) Where it is manifest
that the injury would not have occurred but for the
plaintiff's carelessness, a non-suit is proper.

Davenport *v.* Brooklyn City R. R. Co., 32 Alb. L.
J. 516.

(b) So, also, if there be no evidence of the acts of the
person injured.

Wood *v.* Andes, 11 Hun, 543.
Bowen *v.* Rome, 23 W. Dig. 406.

This, however, is subject to the rule that such evidence may be circumstantial (see page 207, &c.).

Excessive damages. The question of damages is so far within the province of the jury, that it has been held that a verdict will not be set aside as excessive unless it manifestly appears to be the result of passion, partiality, prejudice or corruption ; although it appear to the court much too large.

> Minick v. Troy, 19 Hun, 253; 83 N. Y. 514.

It may be noticed here that the New York Court of Appeals holds that it has no jurisdiction to reverse a judgment in a negligence case on the ground of excessive damages.

> Gale v. New York Central, &c. R. R. Co., 76 N. Y. 594.

FORMS.

No. 1.

Statement of Claim by Person Injured.

To   , Esq., Comptroller,
[*or*, To The Common Council] of the City of   :
Please take notice, that I, the undersigned, have and
do hereby present a claim against the City of   for
the sum of   dollars.

That the facts and circumstances out of which said
claim arises are as follows :

That on the evening of   ,188 , I was
carefully passing along the sidewalk on the south side
of   street, in the City of   , when I fell and
was greatly injured by reason of the icy condition of the
sidewalk, forming an obstruction thereon.

That the place where I fell is between   and
            streets, and opposite the property known
as the   premises ; and that, as I am informed
and believe, the said sidewalk had been icy and obstructed
at that point for a long time theretofore, and such condition was caused or suffered by the negligent conduct of
the City of   and its officers in the care of its
streets and sidewalks.

That by reason of said fall I have suffered great
injuries : that I fractured one or both the bones of my

16   [241]

right leg below the knee ; that I have suffered great pain therefrom and have been and am unable to use the said leg or to walk, and believe such disability will be in some degree permanent.

That said injury happened without fault or negligence on my part.

That I have suffered, and am likely to suffer great loss and damage through the negligence of said city and its officers as aforesaid, and have been put to great inconvenience and expense, and by reason of the premises claim from the City the said sum of   dollars.

Dated

[Signature of Claimant.]

[Verification, where necessary, in ordinary form as for pleading.]

No. 2.

Statement of Claim by General Guardian of Infant.

To   , Esq., Comptroller of the
    City of   :

Take notice, that the undersigned, as general guardian of A. B. an infant under the age of twenty-one years, to wit: of the age of   years, on the   day of   , 188 , and in behalf of said infant, has a claim against the City of   , not arising on contract, but for injuries to the person of the said A. B., to the amount of   dollars, which said claim, with an abstract of the facts out of which it arises, is herewith presented to and filed with the said comptroller of said City of   .

The facts out of which such claim arises are briefly these :

[Describe accident and injury, stating location and nature of defect or obstruction; time and other particulars of accident;

nature and extent of injury; facts showing actual or implied notice and negligence, and absence of contributory negligence.]

That the damages sustained by the said A. B. amount to the sum of   dollars, which sum the undersigned demands from said city, on behalf of said infant, for the injuries received by him.

Dated   .

C. D.,
General Guardian of A. B., an infant.

No. 3.

Claim for the Loss of Services of Wife or Minor Child.

To the Comptroller of the City of   :

Notice is hereby given that I have and hereby present a claim against the City of   for   dollars, damages, for injuries sustained by my wife C. E. [*or*, by my minor son D. B.] whereby I have lost and will lose her [*or*, his] services and have incurred expense for medical attendance and nursing [etc., etc.] and have been otherwise injured to the amount of   dollars as aforesaid.

The facts out of which said claim arises are as follows : [*Describe accident and injury, etc.*]

No. 4.

Claim by Personal Representative.

To the Comptroller of the City of   :

You will please take notice that I, as administrator of the goods, chattels and credits [*or*, as executor, etc.] of A. B., deceased, have and present a claim, etc. etc.

No. 5.
Notice to Law Officer.

Laws 1886, *chap.* 572.   *Notice by person injured.*

To   , Esq., Corporation Counsel
[*or*, City Attorney] of the City of   :
You will please take notice that I have a claim against
the City of   , which was filed with the comptroller of said city on the   day of   , 188 ,
for   dollars, damages for a personal injury
sustained by me on the   day of   , 18 ,
on   street, opposite or nearly opposite premises
known by street number as   , and that I am about
to commence an action against said city to recover for
such injury.

 Dated   .   [*Signature of claimant.*]

 [*The above may be varied to meet cases where the action is
to be brought by an administrator or executor, a husband or
parent for loss of services, etc.*]

No. 6.

Complaint by Person Injured.

*Containing allegations of notice to law-officer and of leave to
sue* in forma pauperis.

[*Court, and title of cause.*]
 Plaintiff complains and shows to the court :
 First. Upon information and belief, that the defendant
is a municipal corporation duly organized under the laws
of the State of New York.
 Second. Also, upon information and belief, that among

other things it is by the charter of the said city made its duty to keep the streets and sidewalks in said city in good order, and at all times properly protected and kept clear from all and every obstruction.

Third. Also upon information and belief, that the street in said city known as   street has been and is much traveled and used by the citizens thereof and others, and is a public street of said city.

Fourth. That on the   day of   , 188 , this plaintiff was carefully passing along the sidewalk on the north side of said   street; when at a point between   and   streets and opposite the house numbered   , she fell, and was greatly injured by reason of an obstruction and the unsafe and icy condition of the sidewalk at said point, the same being, and, as the plaintiff is informed and believes, for a long time previously having been covered with ice and snow.

Fifth. Upon information and belief, that such condition of said sidewalk was caused by the negligent conduct of the said city and its officers in the management and care of its said streets and sidewalks.

Sixth. That by reason of said fall this plaintiff suffered great and permanent injuries, having broken her right arm at the elbow and having been for a long time, and now being, confined to her house, crippled and rendered sick, sore and lame, and has suffered great pain, loss and damage, and has been put to great expense for medical attendance, and has been otherwise greatly injured through the negligence of said city and its officers, as aforesaid, to her damage five thousand dollars.

Seventh. [*Add allegation of service of notice on comptroller or other officer, where necessary.*]

Eighth. [*If defendant be city of* 50,000 *or more inhabitants, add allegation of service of notice on law-officer, thus:*]

That on or about the   day of   , 188 , notice was duly given to and filed with the corporation counsel to the defendant, being the proper law-officer thereof, of the intention of the plaintiff to commence an action to recover for the injuries aforesaid, which said notice contained a true statement of the time and place at which the said injuries were received.

Ninth. [*If plaintiff sue in forma pauperis, add the following:*]

That prior to the beginning of this action the plaintiff made application in due form of law to this court for leave to bring this action and prosecute the same as a poor person; and by the order of this court, made at a special term thereof, entered in   County Clerk's office on the   day   , 188 , such application was granted, and   , Esq., was assigned to conduct the same as her attorney and counsel.

Wherefore, etc.

No. 7.

Complaint by Infant through Guardian ad litem.

Containing allegation of service of claim on comptroller.

Court.

A. B., an infant, by C. B., his guardian *ad litem*, against The City of	Trial desired in County.

A. B., an infant, by C. B., his guardian *ad litem*, for cause of action against the City of   , the defendant in this action, respectfully shows to this court:

First. That the plaintiff is an infant under the age of twenty-one years, and that by order of this court, made

at a Special Term thereof on the   day of   ,
18   , the said C. B. was duly appointed as the guardian
ad litem of said plaintiff, who was   years of age
on the   day of   , 18   , with power and
authority to commence this action and to prosecute the
same as such guardian *ad litem* on behalf of the said
infant plaintiff.

Second. That the defendant is and for several years
next before the commencement of this action has been a
municipal corporation, and as such during all said time
has been and still is charged with the duty of maintaining
and keeping the public streets, avenues, highways and
alleys within its corporate limits in good repair and in
reasonably safe condition for travel by vehicles, teams
and pedestrians.

Third. That one of the public streets or thoroughfares of the said City of   is known and designated
as   street, which for many years next before the
commencement of this action was worked by the municipal authorities of the City of   , and was used as a
public street by the citizens of   and the traveling
public generally.

Fourth. That on the   day of   ,
18   , there was a large, deep and dangerous hole or
opening in the traveled roadway in the said
street near its intersection with   street, which
said hole or opening had long existed and been suffered
to be and remain by reason of the negligence, carelessness
and want of care and neglect of duty on the part of the
defendant and its officers and servants, to wit, for the
space of at least four weeks, during all which time
said   street, at the place aforesaid, was in a defective, unsafe and dangerous condition by reason of the said
hole or opening.

Fifth. That before the happening of the injury hereinafter complained of, the municipal authorities of the
City of   had notice of the said hole in said
street, or from its public and notorious character they

should have had knowledge of said opening or hole, and should have repaired the same.

Sixth. That on or about the   day of   , 18   , the said plaintiff was lawfully riding with his father, the said C. B., in a one-horse wagon drawn by a single horse along and upon said
street; and while he, the said father, was driving the said vehicle, without fault or negligence of the said plaintiff or said driver, one of the forward wheels of said vehicle suddenly dropped into said hole, by reason whereof the said A. B., the plaintiff herein, was suddenly thrown from the said vehicle, precipitated upon the ground, thereby receiving great and permanent injuries to his person by fracturing one or more bones of his shoulder or chest, and otherwise causing great pain, injury and distress, which confined him to the bed for a long time and to the care of physicians, and still does suffer pain and distress from said injury, to the damage of the said plaintiff of five thousand dollars.

Seventh. That on the   day of   , 18   , the claim for which this action is brought, with an abstract or statement of the facts out of which this cause of action arose, made and verified according to the statute in such cases made and provided, was duly presented to and filed with the Comptroller of the City of   , who did not within   days thereafter audit or pay the same.

[*Add, when necessary, allegation of notice to law-officer.*]
Wherefore, etc.

No. 8.

Complaint by Administrator of Infant.

Containing allegations of appointment of administrator, and of absence of imputable contributory negligence.

Court.　　　Trial desired in　　　county.

> A. B., as administrator of the goods, chattels and credits of C. B., deceased,
> 　　　　against
> The City of　　　　　.

The above-named plaintiff, as administrator, &c. of C. B., deceased, complains against the above-named defendant, and for cause of action alleges :

First. That the defendant is, and during all the time hereinafter named was, a municipal corporation, duly organized under and by virtue of the laws of the State of New York ; and that among other things it is and was the duty of said defendant to keep and maintain the streets and sidewalks in said city in a good, safe and passable condition for persons passing and walking thereon.

Second. That said defendant, disregarding and neglecting its duty in this respect, on the　　　　day of　　　, 18　, and for a long time prior thereto, suffered and allowed one of the streets in said city, known as　　　street, and particularly the south sidewalk thereof, at a point just east of　　　street, to be and remain, to its knowledge, in an unsafe, dangerous and impassable condition for persons walking or passing thereon, by reason of a large wooden structure or counter about eighteen feet long, which leaned against the building on the south side of said street, and projected into and upon the usually travelled sidewalk of said street, about three and one half to four feet.

Third. That on said   day of   , 18 ,
between the hours of two and four, P. M., the plaintiff's
intestate, C. B., was on or passing along said
street, at the point aforesaid, and without any fault or
negligence on his part, or that of his parents or guardians,
the said wooden structure or counter fell towards the
north, and into or upon about the centre of the sidewalk
at that point; and, in falling, struck and fell upon said
C. B., fracturing his skull and otherwise injuring him,
from the effects of which injuries he died within four
hours after the infliction thereof, to this plaintiff's damage five thousand dollars.

Fourth. This plaintiff further shows that thereafter
such proceedings were duly had before the surrogate of
Rensselaer county, that on the   day of   ,
18 , letters of administration were duly granted and
issued to this plaintiff upon the estate of the said C. B. ;
that this plaintiff on the day last aforesaid duly qualified
as the administrator of the goods, chattels and credits of
said C. B., and now is such administrator.

[*Here add allegations of serving claim, notice, &c. as required.*]

Wherefore, &c.

[NOTE.—*The following allegation has been made in an
action by an administrator.*]

Plaintiff as such administrator further alleges that
the said   left surviving him his widow, the
plaintiff, who was dependent on him for her support,
besides others, his next of kin, who have been injured by
his said death to the amount of at least five thousand
dollars.

No. 9.

Complaint by Husband for injury to Wife.

Only special allegations given.

II. The plaintiff further states that A. B. was on the   day of   , 1872, and since the year 1857, has continued to be, and now is married to, and is the wife of the plaintiff.

V. And, by reason of the premises, the plaintiff has been and will continue to be subjected to great expense in and about procuring necessary medical and surgical and other care and attendance and services for his said wife, and to great loss of money in the loss of her labor and services, and the earnings thereof, which he otherwise would have and receive ; and, also, to the loss of the comfort of the society and health of his said wife.

Wherefore, &c.

No. 10.

Complaint by Father for injury to Minor Child.

Special allegations only given.

I. That on or about the   day of   , 188 , the time of the injury hereinafter mentioned, one A. B. was a minor son of the plaintiff, being then between   and   years of age.

IV. That by reason of said injuries to his said minor son, the plaintiff has suffered great loss from the want of service of his said son, which, before said injury, said son had been accustomed to render him, and of which he has since been deprived, and from said son's diminished

ability to labor for the benefit of the plaintiff, and has
been put to great inconvenience and expense, and has
suffered great loss and damage for medical attendance
and other expenses, to his damage   dollars.

No. 11.

Complaint against New York City.

Court of Common Pleas
For the City and County of New York.

A. B. against The Mayor, Aldermen and Com- monalty of the City of New York.	

The plaintiff, complaining of the defendants, respectfully shows to the Court :

I.   That the defendants at all times mentioned in this
complaint were, and still are, a body corporate, existing
under and duly incorporated by the laws of the State of
New York, having the care and charge of the said city
and the government and regulation thereof, and of the
sidewalks and streets thereof, and bound to keep the
same in repair and good order, and free from all dangerous incumbrances and obstructions, and well and
sufficiently guarded and in a safe condition.

II.   And this plaintiff further shows, on information
and belief, that   street in said city,
between   street and   place, is one of
the old streets of said city, and for several years prior
to the time first hereinafter mentioned said street had
been regulated and paved and the sidewalk upon the

south-easterly side thereof had been paved and kept in
a secure and safe condition.

[*Allege nature of defect and facts establishing notice.*]

III. [*Allege facts and nature of accident and injury, and
absence of contributory negligence.*]

IV. And this plaintiff further shows that the injuries
aforesaid were cause by the acquiescence of the defendants in the illegal continuance of the dangerous condition
of the sidewalk aforesaid, and by their neglect and
omission to have the same cleaned off and made safe for
persons passing over the same, and that, as this plaintiff
is informed and believes, the defendants had notice and
well knew of the existence of said ice and snow on and
the dangerous character and condition of said sidewalk.

V. And this plaintiff further shows that heretofore
and on the   day of   , 188 , she presented to the Comptroller of the City of New York the
claim hereinbefore set forth, upon which this action is
founded, and that at least thirty days have elapsed since
the presentation of the said claim for adjustment as aforesaid, but that said Comptroller has hitherto wholly
neglected and refused to make any adjustment and payment thereof.

[*Add allegation of notice to law-officer.*]

Wherefore, etc.

No. 12.

Answer by New York City.

*Presentation of claim admitted. Answer to complaint, Form
No. 11, ante. See verification.*

[*Court and title of cause.*]

The defendants answer the complaint herein as follows:

I. They have no knowledge or information sufficient to form a belief as to each and every allegation therein contained, except as hereinafter specifically admitted.

II. They admit that they are a municipal corporation, existing under and by virtue of the laws of the State of New York, and they further admit the allegations contained in the paragraph of said complaint numbered V. [*Presentation of claim.*]

III. Further answering, the defendants allege that, as they are informed and believe to be true, the injuries claimed to have been sustained by the plaintiff, were caused solely by her negligence, and in no way by negligence on the part of the defendants.

Wherefore, &c.

City and County } *ss. :*
  of New York, }

———- ———, the Deputy Comptroller of the City of New York, and an officer of the defendant in the above-entitled action, being duly sworn, says that the foregoing answer is true to his knowledge, except as to the matters therein stated to be alleged upon information and belief, and as to those matters he believes it to be true. Deponent further says, that the reason why this verification is not made by the defendants, is that they are a corporation, and that this deponent is an officer thereof, to wit: deputy comptroller; and that the ground of his belief as to all matters not herein stated upon his knowledge, are as follows, to wit: information obtained from the books and records of the department of finance, or of other departments of the city government, or from statements made to him by certain officers or agents of the defendants.

———— ————,
Deputy Comptroller.

[*Jurat.*]

No. 13.

Answer by City of Buffalo.

Presentation of claim admitted.

[*Court and title of cause.*]

And now comes the defendant, the City of Buffalo, by   , its attorney, and for answer to the complaint of the plaintiff herein, says :

I. This defendant admits that at all the times mentioned in said complaint, it was and now is a municipal corporation, duly organized and existing under and by virtue of the laws of the State of New York, and that the plaintiff herein presented his pretended claim for the damages complained of to the common council of the defendant, and demanded payment of the same, and said common council refused to pay said claim, or any part thereof.

II. And further answering said complaint, this defendant says it has no knowledge or information sufficient to form a belief as to the truth of any of the allegations in said complaint contained, not hereinbefore specifically admitted ; and, therefore, denies the same, and each and every part thereof.

Wherefore, &c.

No. 14.

Answer by City of Rochester.

Public street admitted.

[*Court and title of cause.*]

For answer to the complaint of the plaintiff in the action above-entitled, the defendant admits that it is a municipal corporation, with powers and duties as in said complaint alleged ; that   street, in said complaint mentioned, is a public street in the city of Rochester, and that   was and is, as alleged in said complaint, the wife of the plaintiff.

Further answering, on information and belief, the defendant denies each and every other allegation in said complaint contained.

Wherefore, &c.

No. 15.

Answer by City of Troy.

Nothing admitted but fact of incorporation.

Supreme Court.

C. B.
against
The City of Troy.

The City of Troy, the defendant in the above-entitled action, answering the complaint therein, alleges and states as follows, that is to say :

First. It admits and avers that the defendant is a municipal corporation, clothed with certain powers and charged with certain duties which are prescribed by law.

Second. It denies any knowledge or information sufficient to form a belief as to the truth of any of the allegations of the complaint to the effect that the injuries to the plaintiff complained of were produced or occasioned by any negligence or omission of duty on behalf of said defendant, or of any of its officers, agents or servants at the time when and in respect to the place where such injury happened.

Third. It avers, on information and belief, that the plaintiff's own negligence or want of ordinary care produced or contributed to produce whatever injury he, the said plaintiff, has sustained, and on account of which this action was brought.

Fourth. It denies any knowledge or information sufficient to form a belief as to the truth of the allegations contained in said complaint in respect to the presentation to the city comptroller of the verified claim of the plaintiff, and the facts out of which it arose, and upon which this action is brought.

Fifth. It controverts and denies each and every allegation in said complaint contained, which is not herein admitted or denied specifically.

Wherefore this defendant demands judgment herein for the dismissal of the complaint, with costs.

——— ———,

Att'y for Defendant,
15 City Hall, Troy, N. Y.

Rensselaer county, ss.:

E. F., being sworn, says that he is the mayor of the City of Troy, that he has heard read the foregoing answer, and knows the contents thereof; that the same is true of.

17

his own knowledge, except the matters therein stated to be alleged on information and belief, and as to those matters he believes it to be true.

[*Jurat.*]

INDEX.

A.

[259]

276 INDEX.

WHOLE NUMBER OF PAGES, 332.

www.ingramcontent.com/pod-product-compliance
Lightning Source LLC
Chambersburg PA
CBHW021121270326
41929CB00009B/988